The Afterlife is Real

The Afterlife
is Real

True Stories of People
Who Have Glimpsed Life After Death

THERESA CHEUNG

**SIMON &
SCHUSTER**

London · New York · Sydney · Toronto · New Delhi

A CBS COMPANY

First published in Great Britain by Simon & Schuster UK Ltd, 2013
A CBS COMPANY

5 7 9 10 8 6 4

Simon & Schuster UK Ltd
1st Floor
222 Gray's Inn Road
London WC1X 8HB

www.simonandschuster.co.uk

Simon & Schuster Australia,
Sydney

Simon & Schuster India,
New Delhi

A CIP catalogue record for this book
is available from the British Library

ISBN: 978-1-47111-236-2
ISBN: 978-1-47111-237-9 (e-book)

Typeset in the UK by M Rules
Printed and bound by CPI Group (UK) Ltd, Croydon, CR0 4YY

Contents

Acknowledgements

In today's harsh economic climate getting a book published – especially one focused on the spiritual aspect of our lives – feels very much like a miracle in itself, so I am deeply indebted to my wonderful agent, Clare Hulton, and my inspiring editor, Kerri Sharp, for making *The Afterlife is Real* happen. I am also grateful to everyone at Simon & Schuster for being so very helpful and supportive during the process of getting this book ready for publication – it is truly a joy being a Simon & Schuster author.

As always, heartfelt thanks go to my beautiful family – Ray, Robert and Ruthie – for their love, patience and support when I went into exile to complete this project.

And special thanks go to everyone who contributed their stories to this book. I want you to know that you are bringing comfort and hope to others by sharing your experiences. You are making a very real difference by helping to spread the message that the afterlife is real. You may not realise it, but you are changing and saving lives with your words.

INTRODUCTION

Presenting My Case

Sometimes in a court of law a case comes up that is impossible to prove without a shadow of doubt. There may be evidence to suggest what is or is not the truth, but perhaps not enough proof to remove all uncertainty, and when this happens both judge and jury must rely on witness statements, circumstantial evidence and gut instinct to make their final decision – even if that decision is to not make a decision at all and postpone or dismiss the case. In much the same way, it is impossible for me to prove conclusively to you that heaven is a real place, because, when it comes to matters spiritual, there can be no absolute and definitive proof; but what I *can* do is offer you some pretty compelling and conclusive evidence. Then it's up to you to carefully consider that evidence and make up your own mind.

The aim of this book is to present what I believe to be a convincing case for the existence of an afterlife. The first chapter sets the scene by explaining who I am, where I am coming from and why I felt I had to write this book. At this introductory stage all I ask is that you keep an open mind, just as you would if you were selected for jury service.

In Chapter Two I start presenting my case in earnest with a collection of witness statements from ordinary people who say they know for sure that heaven exists because they have actually died and been there themselves. We will be looking at the amazing phenomenon of near-death experiences. The next chapter will deal with the delicate subject of deathbed visions, when a dying person reports seeing or hearing spirits, or when family, friends or caregivers witness something extraordinary happening around the time of death.

Chapter Four will explore visitations from departed loved ones that don't occur around the time of death but happen in everyday life, and then the phenomenon of spirits communicating through telephones and other technology will be explored in Chapter Five. Chapter Six will discuss some of the most commonly reported signs and messages from the other side and it will also touch on the subject of children seeing spirits, as well as pets and the afterlife.

The final chapter will attempt to show that the death of a loved one can lead to a new relationship with that person in spirit and a reawakening and strengthening of belief. At the very least, I hope it will open a window and let in a shaft of light on the blackness of grief.

The witness statements you will read as I present my case will range from the astonishing to the comforting to the spine-tingling; but, despite varying widely in content, they do have one thing in common: they are all based in fact and not fantasy. As with every book I write I am deeply grateful to everyone who gave me their permission to share their experiences and their integrity. A few sent in their own versions of their experiences, but in most cases I have written up their stories from what I was told or sent, and, when requested, names and personal details have been changed to protect identity. Everyone who contributed touched me deeply with their truth and honesty and asked me to include their story not for personal gain but because they wanted to show others that – even though we may not always see, sense or believe it – heaven is real.

So, if you are ready to read the evidence and make up your mind once and for all whether there is an afterlife, let's begin.

CHAPTER ONE

What If . . . ?

What if you slept? And what if, in your sleep, you dreamed? And what if, in your dream, you went to heaven and there plucked a beautiful flower? And what if, when you awoke, you had the flower in your hand? Ah, what then?

Samuel Taylor Coleridge

The last two decades of my life have been devoted to spreading the word that the afterlife is real. I don't regret a second of those years and, although there have been many crisis points and moments of serious fear and doubt along the way, deep down I have always believed in the existence of heaven. I believe that loved ones watch over us from the other side. They can send us messages and use gentle signs to reassure and guide us. I also believe that this life most certainly does not end with our physical death. We live on. We don't actually die, because the very core of our existence is spiritual and not physical.

My earliest memories of forming an intense and powerful bond with the afterlife began over forty years ago with recollections of my Great-Aunt Rose, a striking but softly spoken lady with brilliant blue eyes. Rose was a medium. She could see and hear spirits. I was very young – probably six or seven – when I started going to her weekly demonstrations. At the time I enjoyed going because it meant I could go to bed later than usual, but I also liked the meetings because it was fascinating to sit at the back and watch the adults. They would typically shuffle into the room looking distant, serious and formal, but then my great-aunt started talking and I saw them turn briefly into people I felt I could like better. Their faces became softer. They started to talk to each other, smile or even cry, and all this spontaneity made them seem kinder and less harsh. What I also recall clearly is that, when the adults first came into the room at the beginning of the session, they never seemed to notice me, but, when the session was over and they were leaving the room, they would suddenly become aware of me. I became important. They would smile or wink at me or even come and talk to me. It was as if I had been invisible before and now I was visible. I was someone worth paying attention to and this gave me such a great feeling.

Sadly, I can't recall much of what my great-aunt said at the meetings. It was the impact of her words on those who attended the meeting that made the greatest impression on me. There are, however, some strong memories – or should I say bright snapshots? – that have lingered and imprinted themselves permanently in my heart and mind. Again, at the time, they didn't make sense at all and made me think that being adult was a very complicated business; but now, looking back with the benefit of hindsight and life experience of my own, I can understand fully why a grown man was reduced to tears when Rose told him that his father in spirit was proud of him or why a young woman smiled and cried when she was told that her baby in heaven was sleeping peacefully now.

Rose wasn't the only medium in my family. My grandmother and mother were both born with the gift, and talk of sensing, feeling and communicating with spirits was the norm when I was growing up. There were, of course, uncomfortable moments – such as the time my mum told one of my school-teachers his departed mother knew he was gay now and she wanted him to know she was fine with that – but there were far more wonderful ones.

So, when you consider that I was born into a family of spir-itualists, my unshakable belief that the afterlife is a real place probably won't surprise you in the least. In fact, you would probably say that I am biased and subjective in my beliefs. I completely agree with you here, but, just because I believe we live on after death, it does not mean you have to believe it, too. My aim is not to convince you that the other side exists but simply to present you with the evidence I have gathered over the twenty-five years I've been writing and researching about the psychic world so that you can decide for yourself. I think it is pretty compelling evidence but, at the end of the day, it doesn't really matter what I think or believe. All that matters is what *you* think.

However, as this opening chapter is largely about my own personal experiences of the afterlife – the evidence I myself can bring forward – it might be helpful at this stage for you to know that, despite my being brought up in a family of spiritualists, it took me close to four long decades to actually make personal contact with the world of spirit, to actually receive proof that there is life after death.

I'd love to say that I was one of those children who could see dead people, like the child in that fabulous 1999 Bruce Willis movie *The Sixth Sense* – but I wasn't. I may have attended spiritual meetings and watched my great-aunt and my mother make contact with the world of spirit and give poignant messages to an expectant audience, but I could not see, hear or sense them myself. I didn't even dream about spirits. In fact, I was completely normal – if there is such a thing. I had plenty of anecdotal evidence from people I loved and trusted but no proof of my own. However, if truth be told, that anecdotal evidence was more than enough for me. I couldn't see, sense or hear spirits and so I simply accepted that I didn't have the 'gift'. It wasn't meant to be. I accepted that heaven wasn't choosing to communicate directly with me, but this didn't alter my belief in an afterlife. I still believed that the world of spirit was all around me. After all, from an early age I had been taught that true faith is to believe without the need for proof. So in my mind I didn't need proof. I thought I just knew. Unconsciously, I may even have been slightly relieved I couldn't make direct contact, as, although the spirit world fascinated me deeply and intensely and was the guiding force of my life, a part of me was scared and not at all sure I could handle it. Like many people drawn to the spiritual side of things, I resigned myself to the role of believer and observer. I wasn't going to experience it at first hand and that was just fine by me.

Unbeknown to me, when I reached the age of thirty-three, my world of trust and acceptance would be shattered. Nothing would ever be the same again. I've told this story many times before, but every time I revisit it there is something new to inspire and guide me. It happened years ago but feels forever fresh and brand-new, like an ever-present reality and a reference point for all my life before and afterwards. Deeply spiritual events are always hard to describe in words because there isn't the vocabulary in this world to describe what is essentially not *of* this world, but I have tried the best I can to convey the essential details to you. I hope they speak to you.

It's me

In the mid-to-late nineties when I was living and working in the United States, I was seconds away from death. I was late for an appointment and driving towards a busy junction intending to turn left. I was feeling frustrated because I was stuck behind two massive, dirty, yellow delivery lorries travelling far more slowly than I wanted to go. Much to my annoyance, I saw that they both intended to turn left, too, so I would be stuck travelling behind them at snail's pace. It was at that instant that I clearly heard the voice of my mother telling me to turn right. The voice came from inside my head but sounded like a real voice. My mother had passed several years previously. The voice was so firm and clear that it was impossible to ignore, and against all reason – as turning right would take me away from the place I needed to be – I turned right. Little did I know at the time that if I had turned left, as I had fully intended to, I would have faced certain death in a pile-up involving a stray dog, a lorry and several cars. The accident killed three people – one of whom would have been me, as it was the driver of the car that had been directly behind me at the junction turning.

At the time I was of course unaware of the impending crash and my irrational decision to turn right puzzled me and then made me angry because it meant I had to travel the long way round to my destination. To make matters worse, as I couldn't get there in time, I ended up missing an important appointment. But later, when I drove back home, my puzzlement and anger turned to shock and horror when traffic slowed to a crawl and I gradually moved closer to the scene of a terrible accident. Right by the junction the lorry I had been tailing had swerved off the road. Several cars – it was tough to tell in the chaos – had crashed into the lorry and each other. The car behind it – which would have been my car – was a smashed-up wreck and the two cars behind that one looked bashed and battered.

For years I had longed for some sign or contact from my mother but I had always pictured it under beautiful and uplifting circumstances – not this kind of tragedy and gruesome horror. Of course, my instinctive reaction was feelings of elation. By telling me to take the right path, the voice of my mother had saved my life. I had not expected to ever experience this kind of proof that the afterlife is real, but here it was. However, later that evening when I turned on the news and images of the accident flashed onto the screen, those feelings of elation gradually began to change to feelings of doubt, bewilderment and guilt. Apparently, a stray dog had run into the road in between the first and second lorries. The second lorry driver had slammed on his brakes and caused the crash. The lorry driver and the dog were not harmed but two as yet unidentified passengers in the car behind it and one in the car behind that had died on impact.

It was when I learned that three people had died – and one of those people could have been me – that I began to distrust my own experience. Rational self-doubting voices began to overpower everything. Had I really heard the voice of my mother or was I just recalling the many times she had told me to trust my heart to help me find the right path in life? Was it just a vivid memory? Or, being an impulsive driver, had I simply got fed up of feeling trapped behind two slow-moving lorries that I couldn't overtake?

And then voices of despair and confusion at the seeming randomness of the accident came into my head. A stray dog had darted into the road and caused so much grief. The dog didn't know what it was doing. The lorry driver caused the accident but not intentionally. His instinct to save the life of a dog was understandable. He was probably a decent and kind-hearted man who listened to his heart, not his head. Was that a crime? He may not have died in the accident but a part of him would have to live with the knowledge for the rest of his life that he was responsible for the deaths of three innocent people – and what of those people? What had they done to bring this tragedy upon themselves? They had done nothing wrong but had simply been in the wrong place at the wrong time through no fault of their own. There was no pattern or higher purpose here. The whole incident – as is so often the case with tragedies and accidents – could have been avoided and was so senseless, seemingly random and unfair. I'd always felt that about accidents but even more so this time when I knew that one of the victims could in the blink of an eye have been me.

As I watched the news that night – although the identity of the victims had yet to be revealed – I thought about their loved ones, and my head and heart hurt with the pain and intensity of their grief and loss. I couldn't stop crying and thinking, Why did they have to die in such a pointless way?

I couldn't stop asking myself why it should be them and not me. There were so many emotions clashing inside me: joy that I was still alive, pain that people had died in my place, anger at the senselessness of it all, but, above all, guilt – guilt that I was still alive when three people were dead.

Emotionally exhausted, I went to bed and slept fitfully, only to awake in the early hours of the morning. I was covered in sweat and my pillows were both on the floor. My bedclothes had been kicked back and were falling off the bottom of the bed. The tears of hurt and confusion started to come again. I thought about those three people and wondered where they were. Were they okay? Yes, I had always believed in an afterlife but did I believe in it now? The sharp and ruthless sword of doubt was cutting my heart into pieces and tearing up a lifetime of conviction. Perhaps the atheists were right and all there is to this life is meaningless and random combinations of nothingness. Perhaps when we die, death *is* the end, and our bodies return to become part of the earth, not heaven.

I had never felt so empty, hollow and alone my entire life. My eyes felt heavy and sore and my body ached. Contemplating the possibility of living the rest of my life without the spirituality that had inspired and sustained me up until this point was shatteringly exhausting, both physically and emotionally. I hit rock bottom. I didn't believe any more. I didn't trust that the accident had happened for a reason. I couldn't accept that there was some higher and greater purpose. With thoughts of emptiness, blackness and nothingness swirling around in my head, once again I fell into a restless and painful sleep.

I'm not sure if it was a shaft of sunlight or a voice that woke me, but when I opened my eyes I saw and heard both at the same time. The voice was so real that I sat up and switched on my light. I looked around my bedroom but there was nobody there. Then I heard the voice again. I grabbed my bedclothes and wrapped them around me. Perhaps I was going mad. After all, isn't hearing voices the first sign? I had heard them twice in one day now – first my mother's voice and now this one. However, although I could have explained away my mother's voice as something that may have been coming from inside my head, this was impossible to rationalise or explain away, as the voice was neither my mother's nor my own. It also wasn't coming from inside my head but sounded as if someone were actually in my room. The voice was that of a young woman. It was songlike and I was sure I could detect a slight British accent, but it was also American-sounding. At first I didn't know what the voice was saying. I just knew she was speaking to me, speaking all around me and within me, but then I could faintly make out what she was saying. She said, 'It's me. It's Jane.' Then she went on to say that I had nothing to be afraid of. She said she was all right and that everything was all right for her as well as her husband, and it would be all right for me, too. Everything would work out fine.

And then the voice stopped. I called out to it but it was gone. I slapped my face and it hurt. I was awake. The voice had been real. I got out of bed and paced around the room. For some bizarre reason I opened cupboards and windows looking for an explanation. I'm not sure what I was looking for. Wide awake now, I went downstairs and switched on the news hoping it would help calm my nerves. I had no idea what time it was and was shocked to see that it was nearly nine o'clock in the morning, a Saturday morning. I sat there for a while, numbly watching images on the screen, and then a wave of over-whelming fatigue and weariness came over me. It must have been a reaction to my sleeplessness the night before and I didn't fight it. I just lay down on my sofa and drifted away.

It was nearly lunchtime when I awoke and the image I saw on the television when I first opened my eyes was the now familiar and eerie one of my near miss on the local news. It was like rubbing salt into a sore wound or hitting a bruise with a hammer. I couldn't face it and searched for the remote to switch it off but couldn't find it, so I got up to switch off the TV man-ually. As I fumbled my way to the TV it was impossible not to hear what was being said and what I heard gave me the shock of my life.

The victims of the crash had now been formally identified: a retired postal worker called Sam and a recently married British couple now living in Florida called Jane and Harry. In an instant I knew without a shadow of a doubt that the voice I had heard in the morning was the voice of Jane – the woman who died in the accident. I really believe I heard her talk to me in a distinctive British-American accent. She told me that everything would be fine. How was this possible?

It is difficult to underestimate the impact of this on me. It was out of this world. I think I must have stood by the television for a good twenty minutes numb with feelings of shock and awe. What had happened to me was something my rational mind would never be able to explain away. No amount of fear, self-doubt and uncertainty could change what had happened. This was for real and this was for life. It felt intensely privileged and humbled to know that Jane in spirit had taken the time to visit and reassure me. I didn't know anyone called Jane and there was no other explanation for the name to reveal itself to me in this way. I hadn't asked for it, but proof of an afterlife had been given to me all the same.

Hearing voices is often considered to be the first sign of madness – and, in the years that followed, it initially made me very apprehensive to discuss or share my story with others – but let me reassure you that I am not mad. I may have my eccentricities and seem a bit dreamy and preoccupied at times but I am no madder than the next person. I never wanted or craved this kind of experience and nothing like it has ever happened again, but it happened. It really happened.

I heard the voice for only a few moments but it was enough to transform the rest of my life. A feeling of peace and comfort came over me, a feeling I had never known before but one that was somehow familiar. The only way I can describe it is like floating in a warm bath after a tough day or drinking hot chocolate on a cold winter's evening. I stood up and made myself something to drink and the feeling of peace and the comfort of knowing everything would be all right continued to wrap itself around me like a blanket. And as I started to go about my daily routines, feelings of responsibility, purpose, resolve and direction also began to envelop me. From that day on, I was going to live a life that would make those who had died instead of me in that fatal accident proud.

I still had no idea why my life was miraculously spared that day and why Jane had to die instead of me, but I did know deep down that Jane and the other people who died were okay. They were on the next phase of their spiritual journey or destiny. And, although I was very nervous and uncertain at first about sharing my experience with others for fear of ridicule, as the years passed a new resolve and passion began to grow within me to share my story – my personal proof that the afterlife is real – with as many people who wanted to hear what I had to say as possible. And that is why I have written this book along with all my other books about the paranormal. I first started writing reference works and encyclopedias about the spirit world, and then, in 2007, I finally came out of my shell and published the first of several collections of stories about angels and spiritual experiences. This book differs from these earlier publications, though, in that it focuses exclusively on afterlife experiences.

Making contact

Now, my passion for spreading the word that the afterlife is real burns as brightly as it did that illuminating day. This book stands alongside numerous others I have written about the spiritual world and each one carries the same message: we are spiritual beings having a human experience and not human beings having a spiritual experience. And the fact that a number of those books have gone on to become bestsellers shows that I am not alone. There are a lot of you out there who believe in the world of spirit or who are fascinated by or drawn to the idea of an afterlife. Indeed, if recent surveys and polls are to be believed, a staggering 60 per cent of us believe in an afterlife.

Perhaps you have your own personal proof of an afterlife and are reading this because it feels like coming home. Or perhaps you want to believe but aren't sure because it hasn't happened to you or you haven't had any signs or made contact. If this is the case my advice to you is not to try too hard. There have been many times in my life when I have tried to make contact only to be disappointed. Far better to keep an open heart and mind, and then one day, typically when you least expect it, you may hear a spirit call your name. You may be a mature adult when that happens, as was the case for me, or you may be much younger or far older. First-contact stories have been sent to me by parents of babies and young children as well as people up to the age of ninety-four! And some of these stories belong to that category commonly referred to as *deathbed visions* (more about them later).

The point I'm trying to make here is that some of us may wait a lifetime to see spirits, or maybe not even see them at all until the very end or beyond the end, but, even if that is the case, it does not really matter. Yes, I've been fortunate in my life to have had glimpses of the afterlife and, yes, many of the stories you will read in this book will astonish you or send shivers down your spine. But my aim in writing has never been sensationalism but to reassure and comfort you that you are not alone; to show you that, even if you don't have any proof of your own, there is more than enough so-called proof out there from ordinary people to reassure and sustain you and give you hope; to show you that it is not extraordinary experiences that can bring comfort or even belief in life after death, but faith in the eternal and indestructible power of love; to show you that, even though you may sometimes feel very alone, the world of spirit has very probably already been reaching out to you in ways that you haven't noticed or recognised yet.

Departed loved ones often use subtle signs and coincidences when trying to tell us they are visiting, and sometimes these signs are so personal and gentle that we dismiss them as meaningless coincidence or think we are making it all up. That has again certainly been the case for me, and the older I get the more I am able to look back on my life with the benefit of hindsight and see connections between the world of spirit and my life on earth that I failed to notice at the time. I'm really hoping that, after reading this book, you will start to look back on your own life and start recalling and noticing these signs and connections for yourself. Perhaps in the months or years following the death of a loved one you met someone or something magical happened that made you feel stronger and better. Perhaps you woke up one morning and the heaviness of grief didn't feel quite so oppressive. Perhaps a beautiful sunset or a piece of music spoke to you and life didn't feel quite so empty and black any more. Whatever it was that lifted your spirits, perhaps when you look back you will start to think of it as heaven-sent.

Having read hundreds of afterlife stories over the years, not only have I learned that there is no age or stage in life when contact with the world of spirit is more or less likely, I have also learned that spirits communicate to us in countless different ways – all you need to do is start looking out for them and believing in them when they happen. And don't fall into the trap of thinking you need to be a medium, psychic, clairvoyant, spiritualist, angel person or deeply religious person to see spirits. The media often like to describe me as a 'psychic' or 'spiritualist' or so-called 'angel expert', and most of the time I'm happy to go along with magazines and papers using these titles because they are easy to understand and grab the reader's attention. But if you have read my books you will know that I have never claimed to be any of them. In fact, it sometimes makes me feel uncomfortable being labelled in this way because to this day I still do not believe I have what is often described as the 'gift' – the ability to see and hear spirits. In my mind I'm just an ordinary woman. Yes, I have had supernatural experiences but they have simply happened without reason or explanation and not because I have tried to make them happen. I can't predict or control them and have stopped trying. To risk repeating myself, I do not think of myself as a 'psychic', or any suchlike, as I don't think I have any special or unique psychic abilities. I think of myself as an ordinary human being with a heart and a mind that is open to the possibility of contact with the world of spirit. Indeed, as this book will make clear, the only requirement for seeing spirits is an open and trusting heart. It took me nearly four decades to understand this vital truth.

One thing I have learned over the years is that the harder I try the further away the world of spirit seems to be and the more alone I feel. I have learned that self-doubts, fears and preconceived ideas of the afterlife shut out any possibility of contact and I don't want you to make the mistakes I did. So, if the only thing you take away from this book is to open your mind to the world of spirit that already lives within and around you waiting to reveal itself when you are ready, then my 'job' will have been done. As you'll see in the pages that follow, the world of spirit can speak to us in many visible and invisible ways. Yes, some people may be blessed with the rare ability to actually see or hear spirits and then there are those extreme cases of people who have actually died and gone to heaven and come back to life to tell their story, but it is more common to smell an essence, feel a presence or sense a shift in energy or experience a vivid and almost lifelike dream of a departed loved one. More common still are subtle, gentle signs and coincidences that can be easily missed if your heart and mind are closed – a white feather, a rainbow, a butterfly, to name but a few.

I have had other encounters with the world of spirit – and if you'd like to find out more you can read about them in some of my other books – but my experience on the freeway remains the most monumental and convincing for me, and that is why I decided to start this book with it. It is my own witness statement. It is the best evidence I personally can offer you for the existence of heaven, because, whether you believe me or not, I know what happened to me was real.

But is the afterlife real?

It's a question we have all considered. When our time comes, is it all over? Is there life after death? And, if there is, what is it like? Is death followed by heaven or hell? Do we become ghosts? Or was Plato right, and do our bodies die but our souls remain?

I am hoping that the stories you read in the pages that follow will at the very least make you think that there just might be more to your life than meets the eye. In the words of great philosopher Nietzsche, 'Even a thought, even a possibility can shatter and transform us.' It is your choice to believe or not to believe – always your choice. All I beg you to do at this stage is to not close your mind, but just start asking yourself, What if . . . ?

It is an encouraging sign that, when it comes to supernatural experiences, a number of scientists today are starting to ask 'What if . . . ?' and keeping an open mind about the possibility of life after death. One of the fascinating things I discovered when researching for this book is that, far from denying the existence of an afterlife, modern science is actually choosing to explore and in some cases even embrace the possibility. At the front line of this research is exploration of the fascinating phenomenon known as near-death experiences, which we will explore further in the next chapter. By studying thousands of detailed accounts from people on the brink of death, an ever-increasing number of scientists and doctors have found themselves coming to the astonishing conclusion that near-death experiences (or NDEs) provide such powerful scientific evidence that it is reasonable to accept the existence of an afterlife. And, NDEs and the search for solid proof aside, science itself is also discovering many things it cannot physically prove but believes to be true – ephemeral matter, curved space, liquid time, to name but a few – and there is no reason why the existence of an afterlife should be regarded as any different. Indeed, from a quantum-scientific perspective, visitations from the world of spirit are simply things that humans have yet to understand well enough.

Quantum science and the testimony of respected researchers and doctors concerning NDEs are compelling evidence, but I'm well aware that there will always be sceptics out there who will try to find alternative and, in their minds, more rational explanations for stories that appear to confirm the existence of an afterlife. However, to those who believe, to those who trust in heaven, no explanation will ever have the power to transform and inspire their lives as the power of the belief they have. Once again, belief is right at the heart of the matter here – and who are we to question or explain away the power of belief to transform lives?

Beauty, mystery, healing and a deeper reverence for the sacred mystery of life characterise all the stories here. Each one is potentially a doorway, a passageway to another understanding of reality, and, if you allow what you read to flow in without judgement, you may be astonished at your own capacity to awaken your soul and embrace levels of spiritual awareness that you were previously unaware of. But, however this book affects you, I'm in no doubt that you will be inspired and energised – as I never fail to be – by the true stories of people leading ordinary lives who have caught a glimpse of something astonishing. And whether you have seen spirits or not, or choose to believe or not, I trust that reading about people whose lives have been transformed will be a truly moving and uplifting experience for you. For my part, working on this book has opened my eyes to new possibilities and given me renewed faith.

Yes, in my opinion and – as we'll see in the pages that now follow – in the opinion of countless other people from all walks of life the afterlife is real. Our departed loved ones are waiting for us there. They are never far away and they do want to communicate with us. All we need to do is listen to them. All we need to do is keep asking ourselves, 'What if ...?'

What if ... we don't die?

What if ... there is life after death?

What if ... heaven is real?

CHAPTER TWO

Eyewitness Accounts

> I think death is a tremendous adventure – a gateway into
> a new life, in which you have further powers, deeper joys
> and wonderful horizons.
>
> Dr Leslie D. Weatherhead

It's unlikely that we will ever have solid scientific proof that there is life after death, but we do have something that comes extremely close, and that is accounts of people who have actually died or been on the brink of death and returned to tell their stories. These voyagers to frontiers unknown report astonishing glimpses of a world beyond, a world that shimmers with light, magic and love. In this chapter I'd like you to meet some of these people and let them take you on an incredible journey to the other side.

Let's begin with this brief but breathtaking testimony sent to me by Hailey.

I Can See Clearly Now

In 2005 I nearly died on the operating table. I haemorrhaged and my doctor later told me that everyone thought they had lost me. I recall floating above my body and seeing the surgeon and staff panic as they tried to save my life. I didn't feel any panic myself. It was as if I was watching an interesting novelty. I wasn't involved.

Suddenly, I felt myself being blown feet first into a grey mist. I don't know why but I remember seeing my legs and bare feet bathed in yellow light floating into the mist. When I was in the mist I lived my life again. Can't explain it very well but I remembered everything and again there was that feeling of interested detachment. I wasn't involved. I just watched. Then I found myself in this beautiful place. It was the most gorgeous and glittering place I have ever seen – like a garden but so much more than a garden. I felt nothing but completeness and happiness. My mind was still. I heard music but music that I have not heard on earth before, and the scenery about me was like nothing I have seen on earth either – it was so vivid and beautiful. It shimmered like crystal and diamonds. Then everything vanished and the next thing I recall is waking up feeling very sore and tired in the recovery room.

Everyone who knows me will tell you that afterwards I changed. I know I have changed. It sounds corny but I feel like I was somehow born again, starting my life again. I am more compassionate and considerate of myself and others. I live in the present. I'm not afraid to be loving and spontaneous. I see more clearly now.

A brush with death

What Hailey experienced falls into that category of stories known as near-death experiences, or NDEs. NDEs are spiritual experiences that typically occur when a person is clinically dead or dangerously close to death. Phrases associated with the experience such as 'go into the light' or 'my life flashed before my eyes' have entered our everyday language and come from decades of research into mystical experiences people have when they are at the brink of death.

In his classic and bestselling 1975 book *Life after Life*, NDE expert Dr Raymond Moody first coined the term 'near-death experience', although accounts of such experiences have been reported through the centuries. As long ago as 360 BCE, Plato's *Republic* told the tale of a soldier called Er who had an NDE after being killed in battle but then returned to his physical body to tell others his remarkable story. Initially, during an NDE there is a feeling of peace and acceptance and this is followed by bright light. The person may feel as if they are outside of their body in some way. They can look down on themselves, typically describing efforts by medical teams to revive them. Many find themselves flashing through a tunnel and they see light at the end of it. In that tunnel they may encounter spirits of departed loved ones. There may also be a life review when they see their lives in flashback and in some cases a flashforward when they glimpse their own future.

At this point many report hearing a voice telling them they need to return to their bodies because it is not their time. On returning to their bodies and their lives, people who have 'died' find that their lives have been transformed. They are never the same again and they live every day as if it were their last. They believe that love is the only important thing because they know from personal experience that it is the only thing you take with you.

There are many questions about NDEs but one thing is certain, and that is that they exist. There are thousands of reports from people all over the world who believe they have glimpsed life after death, and something that surprised me greatly when I began to research NDEs in more detail for my books was the sheer number of people who have reported them. Initially, I thought the experience was extremely rare and I would have a hard time finding people to interview or talk to me about what happened to them. I could not have been more wrong. Over the years the stories have flooded in, and I shouldn't have been surprised, really, because I've since discovered that in recent years a number of polls and surveys have indicated that as many as one in twenty people may have had the experience. That's a huge number!

And the reason many of these people have not talked openly about their experience before is fear of ridicule, or being labelled 'crazy' by doctors or their loved ones; but, fortunately, this trend is starting to reverse as public awareness of the phenomenon grows. Also, with the advance of lifesaving equipment and techniques, it is worth pointing out that many people coming forward today may not have been able to do so thirty or forty years ago, because they would probably have died. So instead of a few isolated stories, as would have been the case decades ago, we now have thousands of accounts.

Not surprisingly, there have been many doubts about the

validity of NDEs, and chief among these is the argument that the experience is simply a hallucination. In other words, it is the work of a dying or medicated brain playing tricks. But, plausible as this explanation sounds, it cannot explain why, all over the world and throughout history, thousands of men, women and children have reported similar sensations during NDEs despite radical differences in cultures and belief systems. How is that possible? Surely, if the experience was hallucination, wouldn't each person imagine something different? Why are there such strong similarities?

Although NDEs don't follow a set pattern, and everyone who has had the experience reports different sensations, over the years I have studied the phenomenon I've been able to pinpoint a number – six, to be precise – of what I believe to be defining sensations associated with them. Some people experience only a few of these sensations while others experience them all; but, even if only one of these sensations is reported, it can be defined as a near-death experience.

Outlined below are what I consider to be six characteristic NDE sensations followed by true stories sent to me by people who believe they have experienced these sensations. It makes a fascinating read and offers convincing eyewitness testimony for the existence of life after death. Read on and see what you think!

1: Out-of-body experiences

The first sensation is often described as an *out-of-body experience*, or OBE. Often, when a person's life is ebbing away, they find themselves floating above their body, looking down at it from above. There may be fear and confusion at first, but these feelings typically subside and are replaced by complete under-standing of the situation and the absence of fear and pain. There is a sense of peace and harmony.

When people have an OBE they often say that, although they are not in their physical body, they have some kind of spiritual body. It is typically hard for them to describe, but there is a sense of being in a different form. At this point there may also be a sense of complete awareness, freedom and individuality. I think that Anna's story below explains it far better than I can.

Looking Down

When I was in my early twenties I was involved in a head-on collision. I remember the bright lights of the approaching car and the sensation of being squashed by the impact. Then I was above the smashed car. I just hovered there while people gathered around screaming. I could see the panic but I didn't feel any myself. I saw the ambulance team arrive and painstakingly take me out of the car. At one point I hovered really close to my body and I could see myself cough. I could see the faces of the ambulance team – the sweat pouring down their faces. I heard them talk to each other. I knew their names. They got my body onto a stretcher and did all they could to help me. The odd thing is that I knew I could help them by going back into my body but I just wanted a bit more time. It felt so free being detached in this way.

You see, a week before the accident I'd broken up with my boyfriend of five years following the miscarriage of our child and was extremely depressed. I hated my job and had gone back home to live with my parents. In short, my life sucked but outside of my body I didn't feel like a mess any more. I wasn't someone with a failed relationship. I wasn't someone who had lost her child. I wasn't someone who hated her life. I was me. It felt wonderful. I felt like I could soar as high as I wanted.

A part of me must have wanted to come back because the next thing I know I am in the ambulance. Later, one of the ambulance team told me that, as I slipped in and out of consciousness, I addressed them all by their first names, even though there was no way I could have known their names at the time. I told them what I had seen after the crash and how I had heard them talk to each other when I was unconscious. They were not nearly as surprised as I thought they would be about what I said and told me that in their line of work incredible things like this had happened before.

2: The portal

The second sensation typically involves a portal, passageway or tunnel. The person feels themselves somehow being thrust towards this tunnel and it is at this point that there is often the first real awareness or sense that this experience has something to do with death. It is often the case during an OBE when a person floats above their physical body in spirit form that the person is not yet fully aware that they are on the brink of death. Once inside the portal, they typically find themselves floating in a dark or misty space. There is a sense that they are travelling through a passageway and heading towards an intense or bright light. Instead of a tunnel, some people describe staircases or a sensation of flying up into space or a point far above earth where they float with the stars and the planets. Here is what Simon told me.

Passing Through

I had a cardiac arrest when I was in the recovery room and found myself floating in some kind of tunnel. At first it was very dark and I was confused and disorientated, but then I saw this tiny light I felt myself being gently pulled towards. I felt myself longing to go towards it. It totally consumed me. The closer I got to the light, the warmer, safer, happier and more alive I felt – if that makes sense. I knew that I was in a place of transition. I knew that something wonderful was waiting for me at the end of the passageway. I got close to the light and the tunnel wasn't dark any more. It was so intensely light and I could hear myself laughing. I was happy but I knew somehow that I couldn't stay. I needed to go backwards into the darkness.

3: Reunions

Once they have passed through the tunnel or travelled through time and space, people often find themselves surrounded by light that is intense and bright, and within this light they can meet up with the spirits of departed loved ones, or beings of light. Communication that is telepathic occurs and there is a feeling of complete comprehension. Josh talks about this feeling in the story below.

Lost Time

When I 'died' I went to this bright and beautiful place and saw my dad. He looked so alive and he spoke to me. I knew it was my dad even though he had died when I was just one year old. My mum had raised me as best she could but a part of me always felt like something was missing in my life. Never knowing my dad felt like there was a hole in my heart, but after meeting Dad I felt whole and the instant I felt that I was back in my body. I know now that my dad is close by and if I need him he will be there for me. I know this sounds crazy – and before it happened to me I would not have believed it, either – but I did meet my dad. He told me that he had always been with me and had watched me grow up but it wasn't my time to join him yet.

Liz sent me this next story.

Field of Dreams

I had an experience about fifteen years ago. I had a hysterectomy and afterwards had a bad bladder infection, which caused me to suffer a rigor. This was when your temperature rises and you shiver and then it continues to rise and you sweat profusely. I was out of it for about fifteen minutes and during that time I was in a field that was brightly lit and sitting there were my mother's parents and they were sitting on a rug having a picnic using all the things we used when we went on a picnic when I was a child. They were talking to each other but I couldn't hear them, and the next thing I knew they had gone.

As I woke up I could see the nurses and doctors talking but couldn't hear them for a few seconds. I've never been afraid of death and this showed me what a lovely place your spirit goes to when you pass over. This was interesting, as my grandparents helped bring me up with my mother when she separated from my father at the end of World War Two. I have read more of your books and they have been passed on to friends who are trying to deal with bereavement, and they have been helped enormously.

4: Life review

We move on now to perhaps the most fascinating type of NDE of them all: the life review. This is when the individual is able to see everything that has ever happened in their life. In a panoramic view they can see how every word or deed – both positive and negative – has impacted the other people in their lives. Everyone who experiences a life review comes through with the certain knowledge that love is all that matters. They also acquire a thirst for self-development and knowledge, as this next story sent to me by Claire illustrates so beautifully.

The Knowledge

On the day I died I had this sensational experience. It has changed my life, or should I say *saved* my life? I'd had a successful operation and was doing well but then, a few days later, I started to feel faint and dizzy. The doctors couldn't tell what was wrong and I slipped into a coma for three days. During that time I lived my whole life again backwards in another dimension. I truly believe I did. I saw myself arriving at hospital and then I watched everything I have said, done and felt in rewind. It felt like seventy years passed but I was only out of it for three days. And I didn't just see and feel my own life: I felt how my words, actions and even thoughts had impacted on other people. I guess I have to be grateful that I experienced more feelings of love, joy and gratitude than feelings of hate, anger and jealousy. I can't imagine how this experience must be like for someone who has had a no-good life. It must feel like torture. It was illuminating and I can't remember the details, but when I woke up I knew beyond doubt that the only thing that was important in my life was love, and everything else was just small stuff. I also had this burning desire to learn.

Everyone who knows me can't believe how much I have changed since my operation. I never used to read a book or have much interest in the news or world affairs, but now I can't get enough of it. I feel like I have so much lost time to make up. I want to know everything. I'm learning to speak another language for the first time in my life since school and I am always asking questions. I want to know and under-stand. I want to grow.

5: Eternity

Many people who have had a near-death experience report the sensation of time feeling somehow different from the time we keep in everyday life. They feel as if they are in an eternal spirit world and there is no difference between a few moments and a few centuries. In addition, to a new perception of time there is also a new perception of space and travel. During the experience they feel as if they can just think something and it will appear before their eyes or they can think of a place and go there in an instant or long to see a loved one and be with that person immediately. They can see what is happening in other locations and, in my opinion, this could be one of the strongest arguments for the validity of NDEs. Even more incredible, when these people recover consciousness they are able to accurately describe what went on in different locations – what was said, what happened and so on – when physically it would be impossible for them to know this information, as they were unconscious at the time.

Silvia's story is a glittering example of this extraordinary and inexplicable ability.

I'm Watching

I want to tell you about what happened to me eleven years ago during the birth of my third child. I lost a lot of blood and at one point my doctor said everyone feared the worst. I died for six minutes before I was resuscitated. I remember hearing this whooshing sound and then I found myself floating above my body. I saw the doctors working hard to save me. I felt no longing to return to my body but I did feel compassion for the doctors. I could see how hard they were working and how much they wanted to succeed.

At one point one of the observing student doctors in the

room left. She was extremely tearful. I felt myself drawn to her and I followed her. She went into a restroom and washed her face. A nurse came in after her and put her arm around her shoulder. I heard their conversation. The student doctor was distraught. It was the first time she was observing a delivery and she couldn't bear it if I died. It was too painful for her because her own sister had died in childbirth and one of the reasons she wanted to specialise in obstetrics was to prevent this kind of thing happening. At that point I found myself pulled back to my body in the next room. I regained consciousness. I was exhausted and eager to hold my new baby but I remembered everything that had happened to me.

A few days later I asked to see the student doctor who had been present during my delivery. When she arrived I told her what I had seen and that she may well have been the reason I felt compelled to return to my body. As you can imagine, she was speechless!

6: Unwilling to return

And this brings us to the final and possibly the most revealing characteristic of all associated with near-death experiences: a certain unwillingness to return. Rather like the feeling you get on the last few days of a perfect holiday or the feeling a lot of us get on Sunday evening before the start of another working week, for many people the experience is so relaxing and happy that they aren't too eager to come back to earth. I'd like to share this next story with you, sent to me by Mike, because it illustrates this so well.

Not Yet

Don't get me wrong, I'm incredibly grateful to be alive and I wouldn't want to leave my family and my children behind for anything. But when I 'died' I didn't really want to come back. I remember watching all the action as the ambulance crew gathered around me. I'd been knocked down by a van and everyone thought I was a goner. My body looked a mess. It was horrible. I saw all the blood and I wanted to get as far away as possible. I did get away. I found myself floating higher and higher and away from my body. I was soaring and it was wonderful. I was up with the clouds and getting close to the sun. It didn't burn me, it just felt warm and relaxing.

I looked down at the earth and it was like I was in an aeroplane. Everything looked so tiny. I loved feeling so light and my whole body smiled. Then, suddenly, I felt myself falling back to earth. I fought it as hard as I could because the closer to earth I got the colder everything felt and the heavier I felt. I didn't want to go back. I really didn't want to see my body again, but, obviously, him or her up there had other plans otherwise I wouldn't be writing to tell you about my experience, would I?

As we have seen, some people will experience all the above six characteristics, whereas some may experience only one. But, regardless of the nature of the experience, for the overwhelming majority it is a truly uplifting one. In over twenty-five years of study I have not come across one account that expresses intense feelings of anger, panic, hatred or violence. In addition, in every case the experiences transform the lives of the people who have them in some kind of positive and spiritually enriching way. This isn't to say that someone who has had a near-death experience suddenly becomes optimistic, altruistic and a joy to be around. Even though they may have a more upbeat approach to life, what I am talking about here is that they find themselves blessed with an ability to cope with whatever life throws at them that they may not have had before. They are better able to deal with crisis and challenge. Their perspective on life changes and they feel enlightened and more compassionate to others. Lily's story speaks fluently about the serenity she discovered within and around herself after she was 'killed'.

Pages

Before I nearly died I was one of those people who always felt incomplete. I was addicted to just about everything: drink, cigarettes and bad, destructive relationships. I'd wake up in the morning wondering how I would get my next fix and increasingly I was finding that fix in a bottle. Ironically, it was a bottle that nearly killed me. I was walking home clutching one in my hand when I tripped and fell. As I fell the bottle smashed and the glass cut deep into my stomach. I can't remember anything after that. I'm told that some good Samaritans found me lying on the pavement and called the ambulance.

I was rushed to hospital and patched up. I died for almost an hour or so I'm told. I can't remember any of it but I can remember floating into this great ball of light, and then, when I got in it, I found myself in this huge library-like place. There were books everywhere and it felt so wonderful to be there. I felt like I belonged. A book came floating towards me and inside I saw pictures of my little girls. They were crying and it was the most painful thing for me. I knew I had to go back. I needed a second chance to be a good mother.

When I woke up all I could think about was my girls and to this day that hasn't changed. My first thought when I wake up isn't drink or fags: it is my girls. I haven't had a drink now for three years and I know I never will. I don't need drink any more. I've seen the light.

After an NDE, in addition to changing for the better, many people say they no longer fear death. I envy that, because, despite my deep belief in an afterlife, I am still very scared of dying. I shouldn't be, but I am. I still get moments when I wake up in the middle of the night with an anxiety attack. I'm guessing that many of you reading this will also have had your moments of fear, doubt and panic about the certainty of death. There can be many different kinds of trigger. Perhaps you are watching a news report about a natural disaster. Perhaps the death of a loved one or someone you know brings you face to face with your mortality. Perhaps you drive past a terrible accident on the motorway on your way home from work. Or perhaps there is no trigger at all, just a sudden feeling of dread, uncertainty and fear. In an instant, death or dying is not something abstract or distant, or something that happens to other people, but something you have absolutely no choice about.

What do you do when those feelings of dread strike? Do you try to distract yourself with frantic activity, or do you ignore how you feel? I can tell you what I do and what helps me. I open my file of stories sent to me by people who have had NDEs and I read them. Stories like this one sent to me by Joyce.

Dying Young

I know that we are more than our bodies. I know that, because I believe that I have seen heaven. When I was twelve I was in a riding accident and doctors struggled to revive me. Sounds strange, but dying young was the best thing to happen to me – I had a vision on the operating table. I floated above my body for a while and then I was in this glittering countryside. I was beside a lake and my grandparents on my mother's side were there with me as was my beloved dog Sandy, who died when I was ten. It was so exciting to see them and I wanted to tell them so much, but they told me that there wasn't time now, I would have to wait. They also told me that, even though they wanted me with them, my life on earth was precious and I needed to live more moments before I came back. At that instant everything disappeared and next thing I can recall is my mother's voice at my bedside.

I'm eighty years old now and I know that I haven't got too many years left in me. When my time comes to 'die old' I know that I have nothing to fear, but until that time I am going to do what I have done all my life and follow the advice I was given in heaven. I am going to live every moment to the full. I going to tell my family and friends how much I love them and I'm going to help others and be kind as much as I can. Dying young taught me that every moment is a gift, and I don't intend to waste a second.

Then there are accounts like this poignant one sent to me by Benjamin, who 'died' from internal bleeding following a fall. During his coma, Benjamin felt his spirit leave his body and travel to the stars, where he experienced visions of universal and overwhelming love, but I have not included that part of his letter here because it is the spiritual awakening following his NDE that I want to highlight.

Was it Worth Dying?

The doctors could not believe that I had survived. Within a week I was feeling normal again, clearer, yet different than ever before. My memories of the journey I had taken when I was in a coma started to filter back. I could find nothing wrong with any human being I had ever seen. I thought of myself as a human again and I was happy to be that. From what I have seen, I would be happy to be an atom in this universe. I'm aware that a lot of what I've been saying doesn't sound logical or reasonable, but I've seen that logic and reason, along with time and separation and differences between people, are illusions. They aren't real. I know that what I had experienced wasn't a hallucination or dream. It had been real. I know that the only thing that matters and is completely real is love. Complete, open, giving and incredibly filling love. That is the only thing that matters. All else is superfluous.

I'm fully aware that my story sounds 'trippy' to say the least. I would have dismissed it as a hallucination before it happened to me, so I completely understand if you don't believe me. I just want you to know that before it happened I'd never been religious or spiritual, but after my vision I was changed for ever. I simply am changed. We are all one. We are the world, the universe, the heavens. I'm no expert but from what I've since read and heard about near-death experiences, although people may describe what they have 'seen' in their own religious terminology, religion is immaterial. The central message is of universal and uniting love, regardless of where you were born and which god you worship; we are all one. I now find myself openly crying over the sadness in the world and in people's lives. If I can somehow relieve another's suffering by sharing it with them I will do so gladly. But I also find myself rejoicing whenever there is joy and laughter in the world.

In a nutshell, I suppose the question many people want to ask me would be, 'Was it worth dying?' I would have to answer, joyfully, 'Yes!'

Reading stories like these can help awaken you to the bittersweetness of your mortality and remind you that, whenever you become aware of the love and compassion inside your heart and around you, there is a doorway to heaven and a stairway to eternity. You will know that you are stronger than death. You will know that you do not need to fear death.

On their return from an NDE, many people also say that

they feel happier to be alive than they have ever done previously, and a key part of this is their absolute conviction that love is the only thing in life that matters. It is the reason for their existence and, as this next story from Steve describes so powerfully, their whole attitude to life changes.

Happy to Smile

I used to be such an anxious, moody and, dare I say it, mean-spirited person before I almost died. I was deeply suspicious of anyone with a smile on their face. But now I'm the person who can't stop laughing. I used to worry about what car I drove, what job I had, who I was seen with and all those things that I now know don't really matter. I'm happy to be seen with anyone. I'm happy to smile at anyone because I know that the only thing I will be judged on is how much I have loved. I also know that everyone is capable of love and deserves to be loved and that we are all connected in spirit.

You can see in that story that, as well as a change in value structure, Steve also returned with a sense or awareness that there is an association or link between all humankind and everything in the universe. This newfound awareness also features in Dani's story.

All About Me

I could write pages and pages about my near-death experience and perhaps one day when I have time I will write it all down; but for now I just want to tell you that following my cardiac arrest last November I had what I can only describe as a mind-blowing experience. I truly believe that as doctors tried to save my life I went to heaven. I left my body and entered this tunnel of light and when I was travelling in that tunnel I lived my life again. It didn't make great viewing, as it was all about me. I longed to see how my life was impacting on others or making a difference to them, but nothing came up. I was just there and people didn't seem to care very much about me. I also got a glimpse of my future, or what I now know to be my potential future. In my future I saw myself looking very unhappy. I was in a flat or house, I'm not sure, and in that house I had every luxury but I was alone, totally alone. I knew that something must have gone horribly wrong with my life.

Anyway, to cut a long, long story short, when I came back to my body and recovered and returned to my life, everything I had ever worked for seemed meaningless. Before, my first thought was always along the lines of, What's in it for me? or, How will this impact me? or, What can I get out of this? But now I was bored of me, if that makes sense. I had had enough of putting myself first. I wasn't interested any more. I was now interested in how I could make a difference in the lives of others. What made me happy wasn't making myself happy any more but seeing other people smile because of what I had said or done. It sounds very *Christmas Carol*-like, but I truly believe that my near-death experience saved me from myself and from a very lonely future.

You can see from Dani's story that she returned with a clear idea of the way she wanted to live her life. She changed her priorities completely. This may in part have been caused by the life review she experienced, as she described seeing and feeling not just her own life but also how her words and actions made other people feel. This experience could have reminded her that everything she says and does has an impact in the world of spirit and one day she will have to review it all again. You might think that such an experience would make Dani paranoid, but I have read many similar stories and this is never the case, because it simply results in the person reassessing their life and making changes to become more careful and thoughtful. This is because greater attention is paid in the life review to the little things we say and do – those simple acts of compassion that come from the heart and that we rarely give a second thought to in our daily lives. For example, one man told me that an image or feeling that came across to him very intensely was of a time when he commuted to London on a daily basis and, even though he was sleepy, he regularly gave up his seat on a packed Tube train to an elderly lady or someone who looked more tired than he was.

Above all, the NDE typically leads to spiritual growth, and by that I don't mean becoming religious or devout. In fact some people find that they no longer want to describe themselves as belonging to a certain religion. It means focusing on what is going on in their heart. This next story explains it far better than I ever could. It's from Gary.

Many Paths

I'm not going to say what religion I was before my experience because I don't want to devalue any religion, as there are many paths to heaven. All I want to say is that I was a devout follower of my religion. It was the centre of my life. But, after I died and glimpsed life on the other side, this is no longer the case. You see, when I was in spirit I saw this bright shining light and around that light there were hundreds of paths, and each of these paths represented a faith or belief system. I also saw spirits simply floating into light without any path to guide them. I knew they were being guided into the light by their hearts. Since my vision I no longer describe myself as religious or a follower of the religion I was born in. I describe myself as spiritual.

Perhaps more than anything else it is the personality changes following an NDE that add validity to the experience. Not everyone who nearly dies comes back changed for the better but, typically, people who have had a near-death mystical experience do. They come back with a newfound love and zest for life, a determination to make a difference and be more compassionate. In many cases they also discover within themselves a desire to focus on the spiritual side of life and, as Gary's story above illustrates, this does not necessarily mean becoming religious.

Yet another factor that can potentially add validity to the truth of NDEs is that they are also reported by young children. Although these children can't possibly have any knowledge or awareness of typical NDEs, all the accounts I have read, including those sent to me by the parents of children as young as three or four, report similar sensations occurring – just as those of adults from all cultures, religions and belief systems do. Even though these children can't have been influenced yet by stereotype NDE information or cultural images, typically there is also that sense of being out of the body followed by a life review – however short – a tunnel and meeting spirits of dead relatives. And, just as with adults, these children often return to this life wiser, happier and more hopeful than before. I'm sure you will find this next story, sent to me by Christopher's mum, Tegan, fascinating.

Standing up

When my son Christopher was seven he nearly drowned. He was at a local swimming pool, tripped and fell, knocking himself out, and then slipped into the water. Thank heavens a swimming instructor noticed quickly and dragged him out. He was able to revive him at the poolside and I believe it was this man's quick action that saved my precious son's life. We took Christopher to hospital to make sure there was no lasting damage and he was discharged after two days.

I noticed a change in Christopher immediately. He had always been a shy and retiring boy with asthma and a stammer, and there had been several incidents of him being bullied at school previously, but all that stopped happening. His asthma cleared up, his speech and schoolwork improved dramatically and he started to become one of the most popular boys in his class. There were no further incidents of bullying, either. His teachers could not believe how confident he had become overnight. I couldn't believe it either.

At first I thought the drama of the swimming pool incident must have been the reason, giving him a kind of celebrity. But then one night as I was tucking him into bed, telling him how much I loved him and was proud of him, he said something astonishing. He told me that his granddaddy was proud of him, too. I thought he meant his granddad on my side of the family but he told me that it was his other granddaddy – the one in heaven. He told me that when he fell into the pool he had gone into a tunnel bursting with sunlight and seen his granddaddy there, and his granddaddy had told him that he loved him and was proud of him. His granddaddy also told him that he needed him to stand up for himself now, because he was special and the world needed to see how special he was.

Ten years later Christopher continues to prove to me and everyone he meets how special he is. Do you think he really met his granddaddy in spirit when he almost died that day at the swimming pool?

Alongside compelling accounts from people of all ages, I have also received a number of equally compelling stories from people who have not had an NDE themselves but who were present when someone was dying and have witnessed something extraordinary happening themselves. As you'll see from Rodrigo's story below, they can also have an out-of-body experience (OBE) and enter a tunnel to travel towards a bright light, and then, after the experience, they find themselves back in their bodies but spiritually transformed.

Overseas

We were on holiday in France and my girlfriend was involved in an accident. She was riding her bike quite a way ahead of me and a speeding car hit her. It was terrifying, and when the emergency services arrived it was obvious that she wasn't going to make it. They tried their best but her injuries were so severe. As I stood there in the road watching them work, I must have been in a state of shock, because suddenly everything started to whirl around me. I lost my balance and sat down. Next thing I remember is floating above the accident scene holding my girlfriend's hand. She was smiling and I could feel her hand in mine. We floated together for a while and then felt ourselves gently being pulled into what I can only describe as a rotating black box. It wasn't frightening, even though it was black and I was very curious to see what was inside. As we got closer I could see tiny points of light in the black box and they shone like bright diamonds. We were both eager to investigate but, just as she used to do in life, my girlfriend wanted to go in first. I watched her float in but, as soon as she did, everything vanished and I found myself staring at the road with my head in my hands. The emergency team were still trying to save my girlfriend so she could be transported to hospital, but I knew she was gone.

Hardly a day goes by when I don't think of my girlfriend and what I experienced with her at her moment of death. I feel incredibly privileged to have been a witness and comforted by the knowledge that she must have loved me a great deal to allow me to share that wonderful moment with her. I miss her greatly, but I know she is where she needs to be and I know I am where I need to be, too. It is not my time yet.

Such stories are a relatively new phenomenon and researchers describe them as *empathetic near-death experiences*. As I see it, they create a huge problem for people who argue that NDEs are hallucinations or caused by brain malfunction. Why would witnesses who are not dying themselves have a similar experience?

I'm hoping that you are beginning to see why I decided to start presenting my case for the existence of an afterlife with a chapter on near-death experiences. It is because I truly believe such experiences offer perhaps the most commanding evidence we currently have for the existence of life after death. They are witness statements for the existence of heaven.

So what is heaven like?

Although I have not had an NDE myself, from my research I have been able to recognise a number of familiar characteristics when it comes to describing what heaven could be like. Something that is often said is that human words simply aren't able to describe what is being seen or experienced. There are no words to explain the beauty, bliss, peace and vividness of the place. Some people talk about stunning countryside where the flowers and trees have colours that don't exist on earth. One person told me that the flowers were singing, and I have always loved that thought. Another spoke of glimmering lakes and rivers. The sounds of running streams, birdsong and glorious music – again music that can't be heard on earth – are also heard. Butterflies, birds and beloved departed pets may also appear to welcome us. The setting is truly like a fairytale and a uniting theme to all these descriptions is that everything feels more alive and vibrant than it does on earth. Indeed, when some people wake up or recover, they wonder if their lives on earth are the dream, because heaven felt more real.

Some people talk about magnificent cities or palaces where there are vast libraries or places of learning and healing. It does seem that the acquisition of knowledge is highly valued and there are opportunities to learn and grow spiritually. Others talk about levels of spiritual reality that seem to match the spiritual awareness a person had when they were on earth. In other words, those who lived with the spirit of love and goodness in their hearts live in worlds of incomparable beauty and light, whereas those who lived lives of selfishness and cruelty have a more shadowy, grainy and darker existence. It is hard for them to see anything with clarity. What is abundantly obvious is that, in the afterlife, material accomplishments vanish and all that matters is what happened in a person's heart and how they treated others. Love and kindness are the only true measures of success and happiness. If someone has been unkind or cruel, they are not punished as such but will experience the suffering they have caused others because everything and everyone in this life and the next is interconnected.

It seems, then, that on earth our thoughts, feelings and actions determine the kind of heaven we will inhabit. What an awesome and potentially life-changing thought!

But are NDEs for real?

If you are still struggling to accept the truth of all this, I do understand. When I started researching NDEs over twenty years ago, I have to admit I wasn't immediately convinced. Although the people who sent me their stories were convinced they were real, and I wanted to believe them, for my own peace of mind I had to look deeply into other possible explanations for NDEs. I discovered that there are several scientific theories that attempt to explain NDEs, and chief among them is that they have more to do with brain malfunction or, in some cases, mental illness. Another prominent and often-quoted theory is hallucination, so let's begin with that.

Hallucination is a mental state brought on by stress, drugs or lack of oxygen. During a hallucination a person is out of touch with reality and their surroundings, but accounts of NDEs suggest that those who have had an OBE are able to accurately report what is going on in their immediate surroundings. Indeed, a number of doctors, nurses or other observers have been amazed at the accuracy with which a person reports back to them about what took place when they were unconscious.

Another argument against the hallucination explanation is their occurrence in people who have what is known as *flat EEG*. The electroencephalogram, or EEG, is a measure of the brain's electrical activity, and a flat EEG – that is, when the EEG reading is a flat line – is the technical definition of death. If something is going on in the brain, there has to be electrical activity, and hallucinations are recorded on the EEG. However, there have been many reports of people with flat EEGs who have had an NDE. In other words, the experience has happened when they are supposedly dead. If they had simply had a hallucination, it would have been measured by the EEG.

Then there is the argument that suggests that an NDE has something to do with brain malfunction. In other words, when the brain is dying it reacts by causing a state of delirium. Disorientation, nightmare visions and confusion are the hallmarks of delirium, and after episodes of delirium people tend to have very hazy memories of what happened to them. However, as we've seen, none of these hallmarks are associated with NDEs, and delirium is not an experience that brings feelings of renewed hope and joy to a person as so often happens with NDEs. In short, delirium is not recalled as a positive experience, and neither is it a spiritual turning point.

As far as the mental-illness explanation is concerned, I strongly believe that NDE has nothing to do with mental illness, because mental illness typically leads to depression and inability to cope with everyday life, whereas NDEs have the opposite effect and are highly likely to lead to a renewed zest and passion for life. Although – as with some forms of mental illness, such as schizophrenia – NDEs do involve a break with reality, in that the person may hear voices or see things or people that other people can't see, in the case of an NDE the person's life is typically enhanced, not shattered, by the experience. In short, they don't lose touch with reality. They stay very much connected with it.

Sadly, the mental-illness explanation has for many years prevented a number of people from coming forward with their stories at the time for fear they will be labelled 'crazy' by doctors, family and friends. Indeed, I've lost count of the number of times people have told me that they feel relieved to be able to finally tell their stories for the first time. It is a significant development that those who study NDEs today are at last starting to move away from the mental-illness, hallucination and dying-brain arguments. In general, there is far greater understanding of it as a spiritual experience than ever before, and that can only be a good thing, because – as I'm sure you will agree from what you have read so far – NDEs are clearly far more than nightmares or evidence of brain malfunction. But before we jump to the conclusion that this means they are real – they actually occurred – I'd like you to take a look at a few more theories.

One of these intriguing theories is that an NDE, with its tunnel experiences and beings of light, may be a dramatic mental playback of the birth experience. Again, I'm not convinced by this argument. Of course, I can't claim to have any memories of my own birth, but if I did I really don't think it would be a spiritual and uplifting experience, as the great majority of births are sudden, dramatic and painful.

It is often thought that only religious people have NDEs.

This is because of the frequent mention of beings of light and the overwhelming stress on the importance of love and compassion following the experience. This is not a plausible explanation at all, because research has definitively shown that people who have NDEs are not always religious and a significant number were atheists who did not believe in anything at all prior to their experience. Also, even those people who were religious often come back from the experience with less interest in their religion and more interest in nondenominational spirituality.

One argument I often encounter whenever I discuss NDEs with my readers is: if NDEs are real, why doesn't everyone have exactly the same experience? First of all, I point out that there are a number of recognisable and remarkably similar traits – I mention the six most common at the start of this chapter – and, even though some people may have only one of them whereas another person may have them all, to me this isn't a problem. Perhaps I can explain it this way. If I went to the cinema to see a movie and another person went to the same movie, we would both come out of the cinema with different views and memories of the film, although, of course, there would be strong areas of agreement. In much the same way, no two NDEs would be the same. There would be similarities in the narrative but they would not be completely the same.

Some researchers have suggested that an NDE is the brain's way of coping with acute stress. Endorphins – the feel-good hormones – are released to help a person deal with pain and trauma, but to date there has been no research to connect extraordinary amounts of endorphins with the recognisable traits of NDEs. In addition, this theory does not explain out-of-body experiences associated with NDEs. Another defence-mechanism argument is the wish-fulfilment one: a person tries to deny the reality of death by creating a fairytale in which they survive. This theory can be discounted because, if it were pure wish-fulfilment, surely people would have different memories from that of a tunnel or a life review. Surely, they would put themselves on a beach in Hawaii or some similar paradise.

Researchers have spent decades trying to explain NDEs from a physical, religious or psychological point of view and, although many of the theories presented have elements of plausibility, to date there has been nothing overwhelmingly convincing. No medical, scientific or philosophical explanation has been complete, and I don't think it ever will be. What remain convincing, however, are the witness testimonies of people who have actually had NDEs. And it would be closed-minded and unscientific indeed not to also consider the possibility that one way to explain them is to say that they are real, that they actually happened.

Light at the end of the tunnel

Although to the people who experienced them NDEs are convincing evidence for the existence of an afterlife, there is no denying that the only scientific evidence we have for their validity is anecdotal or word of mouth. So, without firm scientific proof, should NDEs be taken as evidence that the afterlife is real? Yes, I believe they should.

I believe this for many reasons. Chief among these are the striking similarities among near-death accounts regardless of culture and religious beliefs, as well as empathetic near-death experiences. Then there are OBEs during an NDE when a person returns with an awareness of what went on around them when they died. How is that possible? But far more compelling evidence than all these reasons is the transformative effect an NDE has on a person. Those who have had NDEs have a totally different attitude to their lives when they return. They are changed people. Their lives change for the better.

Science will never fully accept these stories as proof until it gets something more concrete than what we have at present; but the fact that scientists are looking at such stories as evidence for life after death at all is a huge leap forward (see the recommended reading at the end of the book for more about current NDE research and the work of leading researchers). As more and more people come forward to talk about their experiences they are being taken very seriously indeed, and this isn't surprising, really, because, as science advances and answers more and more questions, death remains one of the last and greatest unsolved mysteries. Everybody is eager to know what happens when we die and at present NDEs remain the most enlightening evidence we have that it is not the end of everything but a new beginning – the light at the end of the tunnel.

If more of us believed in the possibility of life after death and a spirit world where the only things that mattered were not money or power or outward show but love, kindness and compassion, just think about the implications on all our lives. Simply being aware of such a world beyond our own would change our attitudes to our bodies, to the world we live in and to everyone we meet. After an NDE many people talk about their bodies as being 'homes' for their spirits. They regard themselves as spiritual beings in a human body and they think of their bodies in a different way. I'd like to illustrate this with this next brief but illuminating story sent to me by Wayne.

Mirror, Mirror …

Before my cardiac arrest and near-death experience I was a semiprofessional bodybuilder. I defined myself by the way I looked, by the beauty of my muscles. Mirrors were my best friend. But, after seeing my body on the operating table, it wasn't me. It didn't look like me. It didn't feel like it had anything to do with me. I had no attachment to it. Being outside my body felt like home.

I'm not mad, but when I almost died I saw my true self for the first time and what I saw had nothing to do with outward appearances. Today, bodybuilding is still my passion. I still take care of my body, but only because it is the place where my spirit lives. I know that true perfection and true beauty isn't a physical but a spiritual thing.

Please share my story with as many people as you can. I see so many young people today struggling and suffering to look a certain way and I want them to know that in the end this is not what they will be judged on. It is what's going on inside that is the true measure of happiness and success.

The greatest gift

As well as reminding us of our true spiritual nature, perhaps the greatest gift or light that stories about NDEs can give us is hope that death is not the end, and when a loved one passes over there will one day be a reunion. There is nothing more painful in life than the loss of a loved one, and, although time and the support of friends and family can and do offer relief, many people have written to me over the years to tell me that reading NDE stories is a great source of comfort. It helps them understand that their loved one in spirit is being taken care of and there is no more pain. It helps them realise that departed loved ones will be there waiting for them when it is their time to cross over. There will one day be a reunion and nothing can offer greater comfort than this.

As this chapter draws to a close, I trust that the first batch of evidence I have presented to prove my case that the afterlife is real will show you that what we understand as death is simply a crossing over to the world of spirit. Perhaps after reading it you will fear death less and enjoy every moment of your life here on earth more. Perhaps the true accounts here will have reminded you of something you instinctively know already, but may have forgotten along the way – and that is that there is an eternal purpose to your life and that purpose is to remember the importance of love.

CHAPTER THREE

Life at Death

When it is dark enough you can see the stars.
Ralph Waldo Emerson

If near-death experiences aren't quite enough to convince
you that we live on after our earthly bodies have died, perhaps
the stories in this chapter will. Many of the accounts are similar to NDEs in that they occur when a person is close to
death, but they differ dramatically in that the person is not
technically dead when they occur, and, unlike the case with
NDEs, the person does not recover and return to their life but
passes away.

Parting visions

For hundreds of years visions of departed loved ones coming to
the dying to offer love, support, help, advice and guidance as

death draws close have been reported from all different cultures, nationalities and religions. In a typical deathbed vision – if anything can ever be described as typical when it comes to supernatural or mystical experiences – beings of light and/or apparitions of departed loved ones appear to the dying person a few days, hours or moments before their death. Here is Joseph's story.

Tucked In

Mercifully, my wife died in her sleep and there was no pain or stress. I was with her at the end and before she shut her eyes for the last time she asked me why so many people were there. I didn't understand, as I was the only one in the room with her, so I just squeezed her hand tight to reassure her. I didn't say anything. She then told me that she could see her mother and father and her best friend Sally and they were all sitting on her bed. My wife asked me how I had managed to get everyone together and thanked me for doing that for her. I was very confused, as both her parents were dead and Sally had passed over ten years previously. I put it down to the effects of the medication my wife was on and decided not to challenge or contradict her and simply sat quietly listening.

In the next ten or so minutes my wife 'talked' to her parents and Sally. I heard her ask Sally about her children and ask her dad if he was taking care of Mum, as her mum had been wheelchair-bound in the last few years of her life. After she asked a question I could see her nod and react just as if someone was speaking to her. It was very surreal witnessing this invisible conversation. Eventually, my wife turned to me and said that her parents wanted her to sleep now, as they didn't want her to exhaust herself. I agreed and kissed her on the cheek

The last memory I have of my wife alive is her falling asleep with a smile on her face, like a contented child tucked in by loving parents. I don't know what she saw or if she imagined it all. All I know is that whatever happened made her death a graceful and peaceful affair and for that I am eternally grateful.

Samantha had a similar experience.

With Me

Just before Nan died she told me that my granddad was with her. She said she could see him pacing backwards and forwards in the room, just as he always used to when he was alive. She said that he told her heaven was waiting and there was so much for her to see and do. She'd been anxious and fretful before she told me this, but afterwards she was settled and calm and her death was a gentle one.

Wendy believes her brother witnessed something extraordinary before he died. In this story it is not departed loved ones but beings of light – which some people refer to as angels – that appear to ease her brother's transition to the other side.

With Open Arms

My brother Steven spent several months in hospital in 2009. One time he was in the Critical Care Unit and he told our mum that he had seen a lovely young woman in a long white dress standing just outside his room. None of the nurses took any notice of her. She smiled gently at him but never spoke. He said she made him feel very safe. Steven was adamant that he hadn't dreamed her or made her up. He saw her a couple more times and later asked Mum if he was dying.

Steven died on 6 February 2010, just after his 52nd birthday. Steven hadn't been able to lift his arms for several weeks and had been in a coma for several days. He had shown no sign of knowing we were there, even though we talked to him and told him we'd miss him, but it was okay to go if he wanted. Just before he passed Steven got restless and then lifted his arms. I said to Mum it looked like he was greeting someone. About a minute later he left us. When we talked to one of Steven's friends about his passing and how gentle and peaceful it had been, he told us that it was their belief that when you died an angel would greet you with open arms and welcome you to heaven. We know Steven was welcomed by someone and that he was happy to go. We were so grateful that, after the months of pain and trouble, his passing was so incredibly peaceful.

Katie also has this story to share.

All in White

In 1996 my husband, Graham, was diagnosed with cancer – it was an unusual type of cancer and normally found in people that had worked in the benzene industry all their lives and normally made its presence known when the person was, at least, in their seventies. Graham was just fifty-one and the nearest he had ever come to benzene was when he put petrol in the car. Without us knowing, and judging by its size, he had had this cancer for over twenty years! He had suffered from bouts of bad depression and had had various courses of treatment, both medical and psychological, to help him over the difficult times. The doctors thought that when the tumour released its chemicals, that was when he had the depression.

Graham was admitted to hospital on Tuesday, 30 April, for minor treatment – to drain fluid from a lung – and should have been home in a couple of days. When it became apparent that there was something extremely wrong, as the fluid couldn't be cleared, the hospital carried out numerous tests and found the cancerous tumour on his kidney. We were told on 14 May. Graham gradually became weaker as the cancer spread into his spine and on the last day into his brain. He slept most of the time, but when he was conscious he would ask me questions that I thought that I could not answer, as I opened my mouth to say that I didn't know, words came into my mind from somewhere and I was able to give him the comfort he needed.

A week before he died, he said that someone all in white with a white mask on their face had come to see him and told him that he would die, that night/soon, and not to be afraid. I had expressly asked for Graham not to be told he was dying so I asked the nurse who the doctor was who had told him, as she had been sitting about ten feet away, but she said that no one had visited Graham.

Graham died, quite unexpectedly, on 12 June. He couldn't cope any more and I truly believe that the angels knew this and decided that his time on the earth should come to an end. Whenever I visit his grave, the branches on the trees in the churchyard always sway even on the stillest day and I feel a warm breeze around me.

The fact that those who are dying report such visions, and witnesses to the event can actually see them apparently communicating with the other side and can see how this invisible communication brings remarkable changes to their composure and state of mind, is astounding. And before you dismiss all this as pure fantasy, I urge you to consider cases that show not only that visions experienced by the dying are most typically of departed loved ones but also that some dying individuals receive visits from family members they did not know had died at the time. How can that happen? Also mind-blowing is that visions of the dying person saying goodbye to loved ones not present at the deathbed itself have also been reported – more about them later. And then there is the fact that in some rare instances the person experiencing a deathbed vision may have no awareness of their imminent death at all.

Research has also indicated that a lot of reports of deathbed visions don't actually come from the person involved or even loved ones present at the scene, but from doctors, nurses and carers working in hospitals or hospices. These people obviously have a duty of care to their patients but they do not have the intense emotional bond that family members and friends would have, so the question here is: why would such experiences happen to them?

Jack, a hospice worker with over thirty years' experience caring for the terminally ill, sent me this email.

Way of Life

In my line of work death is a way of life. When I first started in hospice care I was quite young and sensitive but after a while I started to feel more comfortable around the dying, and one of the reasons for my more relaxed approach was an experience I had the very first month I started work. I'd been involved in the care of a lady I will call Judith. She wasn't an easy patient, always complaining, and a lot of the staff didn't like spending much time with her. She never had any visitors, and, being young and earnest, I thought I could make a difference and sat with her as often as I could during visitor hours. She was having none of it and told me to leave her be. After a few days of this she realised that I wasn't going anywhere, so she quietened down a bit. Sometimes the two of us would just sit in silence together.

One afternoon as I was coming in to check on Judith, she grabbed my hand and told me that I didn't need to sit with her any more because they were with her now. I asked her what she meant and she said that her sisters and brothers – she came from a family of eight and all had passed except her – were taking good care of her. Then she touched my face and thanked me. It was the first sign of tenderness I had ever known from her. I just smiled and told her I would check in on her later that evening.

A few hours later I came back to see Judith and she was quietly asleep, breathing deeply. I gave her room a little tidy-up but then I felt this sudden and strange stillness wash all over me. Hard to say, but everything went quiet – eerily quiet. I couldn't even hear or feel my own heartbeat. Then I noticed that Judith was suddenly sitting up in her bed with her arms stretched towards the back wall. I wanted to go over to her but I couldn't move. My feet were rooted to the spot. I saw this shaft of bright light fall over her bed. The light made her face glitter and she looked radiant. The light got brighter and brighter and at one point was so intense that I had to shield my eyes. When I looked again everything was back to normal and Judith was lying in her bed again. I went over to her and, from the silent, peaceful expression on her face, I knew that she had gone.

This was not an isolated incident. About six months later something very similar happened when I was present at the death of a man I will call Jacob, only this time I saw swirling lights and heard the sound of flapping wings. I would say that on average I witnessed something magical like this about twice a year and the experience has become so familiar that I don't even question it any more. Whenever it happens I know that one of the residents will die but it doesn't fill me with dread. Quite the contrary – it makes me feel incredibly comforted and privileged.

When I feel it will bring comfort to grieving loved ones I do try to tell them what I have seen happen at the point of death. Reactions vary. Some people are deeply moved, whereas others think I am one sandwich short of a picnic. It's up to them what they think. I see myself as the messenger. I never asked to be able to see what I see, but it happens all the same.

Amanda was also often present at the bedside of the dying during her nursing days. Here is what she wrote and told me.

Talking in Your Sleep

You'd be surprised how many nurses have seen incredible things when a person dies. I was on a night shift when it happened to me and I will never forget it. I was doing my rounds one night when I heard this patient talking quietly in his sleep. I came over to him to check that he was okay and when I came over I could see that he wasn't asleep at all. He was wide awake. He told me that he was surrounded by angels. I checked to see if he had a fever but he was not delirious. I offered him a glass of water and asked him to sit up so I could adjust his pillows.

He was too weary to sit up, so I made him as comfortable as I could and then turned to leave, but, as I did, I had this sudden and unprompted feeling of elation and pure joy.

The whole ward seemed ablaze with light and colour. It was as if someone had switched all the lights on and decorated everything with Christmas lights. It was a large and busy ward and I could see everyone lying in their beds clearly. Then I felt my arms rise slowly outwards on either side of me, like a child who is pretending to be an aeroplane. I felt so light and free at that moment, as if I could really fly, and then in a flash everything was back to normal and my arms fell down to my sides again. Everything was quiet and still and dark in the ward again.

Moments later there was nothing but noise and confusion. The ward sister was drawing the curtains around the man's bed and a crash team had arrived. They tried for a long time to revive him but I knew that they were not going to succeed. I knew heaven had come to collect him and he had gone to a better place.

Although I have never experienced something as remarkable as Amanda talks about here from my time working in an old people's home, I am not surprised at all. In my late teens and early twenties I spent several years working as a carer, and the saddest part about that job was that residents would die while I was on a shift or I would come back to work in the morning to be told that a familiar face was no longer with us. Obviously, when the time for passing came, I, not being a relative or medical expert, would not be allowed to remain in the room, but I would be there in the hours leading up to passing. In those hours I would often notice how calmness come over the dying person, and, with zero change in their medication, there was no obvious explanation for why this should have happened. Sometimes they would talk to me as if I actually were a deceased loved one – typically a spouse or sibling or child – and I would go along with it, hoping that it brought some comfort. They might also start talking to themselves as if they were having a conversation with someone, and again I would dismiss it as the medication or dying process talking. Looking back now, I wonder if they were actually seeing spirits.

On one occasion, I witnessed something really astonishing: a dying man called Brian who had never expressed any interest in poetry all his life started to recite Shakespeare sonnets with astonishing accuracy (I knew this to be so, because I was studying English literature for my A levels at the time). In my research I have since discovered that reciting verse or song when death is near is not an isolated incident and is known by the medical community. There are a number of similar reports and, although not as frequent an occurrence as near-death experiences or deathbed visions, they happen often enough to count as a mental and medical phenomenon that has yet to be solved. I can't explain it but have my own thoughts. Poetry and song are both expressions of feeling. In poetry and song it is not only the words that matter but also how they sound and the feelings they express. So once again at the point of death – on the very edge of life – matters of the heart come to the fore.

In my opinion, deathbed visions stand alongside NDEs as tantalisingly convincing evidence that there is some form of life after death. In many instances the person dying does not appear to be hallucinating or in an altered state due to medication.

At this point I'd like to draw your attention to a major study carried out in the 1970s by Dr Karlis Osis for a book called *At the Hour of Death*. In this classic text, Dr Osis explored studies and interviews with more than a thousand doctors, nurses and loved ones who attended the dying, and he uncovered several important similarities. As well as coming to the conclusion that the person is not hallucinating and is clearly aware of their surroundings when the experience occurs, it was also found that whether or not a person believes in an afterlife is immaterial. In almost every case, dying people report seeing loved ones who have crossed over, and they tell them they are there to help them make the transition to the world of spirit. The dying person is typically reassured and comforted by these visions and in some cases for a few hours before their death their health may even be temporarily restored or their pain relieved.

I've had dozens of stories sent to me about this temporary recovery phenomenon. Indeed, as I was writing this chapter, an email from a lady called Susan appeared in my inbox. Susan told me about the death of her mother who suffered from dementia. In her email she spoke movingly of her mother's final moments and marvelled at how lucid she suddenly became – remembering who her daughter was for the first time in seven years and telling her eloquently how much she loved and valued her. Susan described the experience as 'a miracle, a gift and one I will never forget'.

Many scientists stick with the theory that deathbed visions are simply by-products of a brain deteriorating – a kind of sedative or painkiller to ease the process of dying – but, as we saw earlier, this just does not explain cases where another person present at the deathbed (in particular, someone who is emotionally detached from the person, as is the case with hospice and hospital workers) believes they too have witnessed something not of this world. It also can't explain remarkable experiences like this one sent to me by Leah.

It's Never the End

My father passed away on the 23 May 2010. The week before he passed, we all decided that there would be someone with him at all times, so he knew we all loved him and he wouldn't be left alone. A few days before our dad passed away it was my turn to spend the whole night at the hospital. I sat in the chair beside him, holding his hand, and even though he wasn't conscious he would mumble words, and I made sure, no matter what, I would write down every incoherent word, thinking he may be telling us something important before he passed. This night was particularly bad, as I have heard about the smell of death, but, unless you have experienced such a thing, there is no way of describing the smell. Even so, I refused to give in to the distressing smell and refused to leave his side. Even the nurses tried to tell me they would look after him and told me to get some sleep. I didn't listen to them and stayed until nine in the morning, when another family member arrived to take over.

Feeling exhausted, I went to the motel nearby to try to sleep. This was impossible, as there were people coming and going. So I decided to go to the local club for lunch and a beer (my dad's favourite drink). There was a horse paddock at the back of the hotel. At this time I was at the lowest I could ever remember feeling. I was shocked at some of my family's behaviour during the long week we were there. My brother and sister had not spoken in years and their petty squabbling was just getting me down.

I walked to the nearby horse paddock. Being near the horses made me relax and gave me some much-needed time on my own. I had just walked there when I heard a text message come through on my phone and, thinking it was most likely my sister, I ignored the message, as we had been arguing a lot recently and I didn't feel I could cope with more stress. However, a few minutes later curiosity got the better of me and I checked the message, and it was my brother telling me to get back to the hospital quickly. However, as I turned around to run towards the hospital I found I couldn't move at all and the grass surrounding me had grown, blocking me from going anywhere. I let out a scream and fell to the ground in despair. Then, all of a sudden, I felt a warm light surround me and my dad was there talking to me. I couldn't see him but he was talking to me.

Dad told me I needed to go with him. I 'walked' with him towards the hospital. I saw my stepmother and I went up to her and told her not to be frightened. I put my hand over her heart and said that Dad wants you to know he loves you with all his heart and soul. I could see she was absolutely shocked with what I'd just said. I kept trying to reassure her that everything was okay and, although I couldn't see Dad, he was right beside me. Then Dad guided me to my brother and I told them not to be afraid because

I had Dad with me, and then I put my hand on my brother's stomach (I had no control over what I was doing, but I felt the most euphoric/beautiful sensation during this experience; words can't describe it). I then told my brother that he and my sister have to put their differences aside for the sake of the family.

After talking to my brother I went to sit in the rose garden memorial next to the hospital and Dad was still an invisible presence by my side. He asked me if there was anything they can do. During the week he had tried to ask me a few times if it was the end, but we were instructed not to tell him he was dying. Our father was such a strong man and hated people lying to him, and always knew when someone was, so I told him that the cancer was now all in his chest and there wasn't anything else they could do and that it was all right for him to go now. I kept saying to him, 'See, Daddy, see how beautiful it is,' and that everything has been taken care of. Surprisingly, while I was telling him this, we were both calm and even joking with each other as we always did in life. Then all of a sudden he wasn't there any more and the beautiful light disappeared also.

Eventually, I decided to go back to the hospital and felt remarkably refreshed and calm. Arriving back at the hospital, I was told that my brother had just stood up to his meddling wife (who was the cause of the rift between my brother and sister). He had never stood up to her before and by him doing that he had made my sister realise that he did love her and from there they were starting to mend their rift. At the hospital I went into the kitchen and I saw a nurse called Paula, who hadn't been on duty all week, and I asked her if all families fight when someone is dying. She said it was very common. I don't know what made me say this to her but I told her I thought I'd lost my mind and then I started crying.

Paula took me into another room and I told her about what had happened with Dad and being at the paddock trying to get out of the long grass etc. She then said that she believed in matters spiritual and I had a telepathic connection with my dad and perhaps the feelings of bliss I experienced were what Dad would experience when he passed over. I was shocked, but then Paula's beeper went off and I returned to my dad's room, only to find he was outside in the courtyard, literally going mad at my brother. He was telling him to stop fighting. Whenever my brother and sister fought they were never in Dad's room, but he knew what was happening, which in itself was remarkable. There were two nurses (one was Paula) on either side of him and my brother was in front of him. I was sitting at the table also. After Dad had finished going mad at my brother, he looked directly at me and said, 'I just want to go to sleep because it's beautiful, isn't it, Buttons?' – a nickname my dad always called my sister and I. I was stunned, but the most peaceful feeling came across me. I just smiled back to him and said, 'It certainly is, isn't it, Dad?'

The next day I just stayed away from my brother and sister in the hope that they would work it out. That night we were in Dad's room and my brother and sister walked in together. They were laughing and genuinely getting along. I couldn't believe it. The biggest smile came across my face. I took my dad's hand and quietly said to him, 'See, Daddy, I heard you, you did it. See, they're getting along, all is good now, you can go now.' And, even though he wasn't conscious, I knew he heard me because he gripped my hand.

Dad passed away about eight hours later, just as he said he wanted: with his kids asleep. He didn't want us to see him pass.

The day dad passed family and friends all gathered at his house and it was a very clear night, then someone came inside and said to everyone to go look at the sky. We went outside and there was a cloud in the shape of a halo similar to the light that engulfed me when having the experience with Dad. It was only over the house and about fifteen people witnessed this unusual cloud and we were all just in awe of it. Another incredible thing happened at Dad's funeral. A letter to his wife – my stepmother – was read out and in it he said, 'I love you with all my heart and soul.' No wonder she had looked so shocked when I told her that at the hospital.

I hope you find something in this to help other people who are grieving over a loved one. It's never the end!

Although Leah's father wasn't dead when she had her inexplicable supernatural encounter, it once again shows that, when death is close, the boundaries between the physical and spiritual begin to blur, allowing heaven to shine through.

And, if stories like Leah's, or those from hospice and hospital workers who have no reason to imagine their experiences, are not convincing enough, then visions of a dying person appearing to loved ones who are unaware at the time that death has occurred have to be put forward. This next story sent to me from Ella can certainly counter the grief-induced-hallucination argument as an explanation for deathbed visions.

Sinking

When I was nineteen I was engaged to be married to James. He was the love of my life. We had arranged to meet outside a cinema to see *Titanic*. I knew it wasn't going to be his kind of film, as he was more into war movies and thrillers and things, not historical romance, but I really wanted to see it, as everyone was talking about it. We arranged to meet at six in the evening but he didn't show up. I was upset, but then he called to tell me that he was stuck at work and wouldn't be able to get there in time. He said I should just go ahead and see it without him and he would meet me for dinner afterwards. I was put out but knew how demanding his job was with unpredictable hours – he was a catering assistant – so told him it was okay. He told me he loved me and I returned his love and said I would tell him all about the movie when we had dinner. The last thing I remember is him laughing and groaning as I hung up the phone.

I went to see the movie with a box of chocolates to keep me company. The cinema wasn't very full, so I felt a bit self-conscious on my own, but when the movie started I forgot about everything and got lost in the movie. When it came to that scene at the end of the movie when Jack dies, leaving Rose behind to survive in the icy water, I couldn't stop crying, and I wished James was there to hug me. I felt really low, but then James suddenly came and sat down beside me. I was on cloud nine. He didn't say anything; he just held my hand and let me rest my head on his shoulder. I was so very happy and assumed he must have finished work earlier than expected, bought a ticket and crept in. I could feel him stroking my hair and it was the most comforting experience.

When the movie finished and the lights went up I could not have been more surprised. James was nowhere to be seen. I thought he might have gone to the toilet or somewhere, so I waited in the reception of the cinema for ages. He didn't show. I switched on my phone to call him and noticed there were countless messages. I soon found out that all the messages were from James's mum begging me to call her. Apparently, James had left work on his motorbike around eight and on his way home to change for dinner he had been killed in a collision involving a car and a bus.

Unprompted appearances by a person who has just died are not a new phenomenon: they have been reported for hundreds of years and they are so astonishing that I want to include a couple more stories here. Both are united by the theme that the person who sent me the story was *not* present when the death occurred and they were sometimes in an entirely different location or country. Despite this, at the exact moment of death they all had a vision or some kind of experience that is truly impossible to explain. The stories sound incredible and I can see why you may have problems accepting them as truth. All I know is that the people who sent them to me sounded perfectly articulate and ordinary. All they wanted was for their stories to be shared with others in the hope that they would bring comfort. I had no reason to distrust them, as there is no financial reward for getting a story published in this book, and a number of people do ask me to change their names to protect their identity, so it isn't about attention-seeking either. Read on and see what you think and, as you read, listen to what your heart tells you. Here is Kieran's story.

Flying Visit

My mum died when I was on my gap year before university. I was having the time of my life and I wasn't as diligent as I should have been keeping my mum informed of my whereabouts. Every time I phoned her I could sense how worried she was and I tried to reassure her. The last time we spoke I told her that I was staying in an apartment in Paris with some friends of our family and I intended to stay there for a few weeks.

Three days later I was alone in the apartment when the doorbell rang. I opened the door and Mum came in. Don't get me wrong – I was happy to see her but I was also a bit upset as this year was supposed to be all about me becoming independent. My mum told me that she knew she shouldn't have come but she just missed me so much. She said it was a flying one-day visit and she didn't want to stay long because she was going to do some shopping and sightseeing before she went home. I offered to go with her but she said that she really didn't want me cramping her style – I remember how this made me laugh at the time – and that she would be fine. We hugged and she left, and as I waved goodbye I remember thinking how much I loved her and how I had the best mother in the world, even if she was a bit overprotective at times.

About ten minutes after Mum had gone, I got a call from Dad. He was incoherent. Eventually, I found out that Mum had died thirty minutes ago from a sudden and as yet unexplained cardiac arrest. I told Dad that this was impossible as Mum had just been to visit me, but I don't think Dad understood a word I was saying. He was so tied up with his grief.

This happened twelve years ago and I often wonder if I imagined it, but each time I come to the same conclusion – I did see Mum that day. She did come round to check up on me one last time. The most precious thing is that she looked so alive. She visited me in spirit but to me she felt alive and to this day I still sense her living presence all around me.

Here is Daisy's memorable story.

Wild Horses

It was a Tuesday morning and summer holidays for the children. It was raining outside – typical British summer – and I really didn't know how I was going to keep the kids happy. They were climbing the walls already and noise levels were so high – it was only nine-thirty in the morning. I'd got a thousand-piece puzzle out for us all to get to work on and quieten down but nobody was interested.

The doorbell rang and I thought it was the postman but it turned out to be my dad. I was so happy to see him as we lived about four hours away from each other and, as his health was declining, he rarely visited our house any more. The kids were delighted, as they loved his sense of humour and his stories. He had always been so great with them. So I went into the kitchen to make some coffee for us and milk and biscuits for the children. When I came back into the living room I could not believe it. [Their] granddad was sitting in a chair and the kids were at his feet busy sorting out the pieces of the puzzle into those pieces which had straight edges and those that did not. The peace and silence in the room was like paradise after all the noise and drama of breakfast.

My dad stayed the whole morning and with his help the puzzle was almost completed. It was a beautiful puzzle with pictures of wild horses running in a field. At one point I must have fallen asleep, because when I woke up my dad had gone and my children were watching TV. I asked my kids when he had gone and they told me that when the puzzle was finished he didn't want to wake me and had let himself out.

That evening my mum called to tell me the devastating news that Dad had passed away. I told her that was impossible because he had visited me that morning to play with the children. We both choked back the tears and later that night, when Mum came round to stay with us, I showed her the puzzle and asked the children to tell her who had helped them finish it. They told her all about Granddad's visit. My mum was speechless at first and almost fainted. Later I found out that the last thing Dad said her to before he passed was, 'horses running free'.

Daisy's story is fascinating because, unlike those in many of the stories in this book, she was not the sole witness. Her children also spent time with their grandfather in spirit.

Stories like this are intense and dramatic because they involve a full-blown vision of a deceased loved one at the moment of death. But such stories are extremely rare. More usual are those sent to me from people who didn't have a vision but had a surreal experience when an absent loved one died. Sometimes this was a sensation of being kissed, a breeze or rush of wind, a shaft of light or something else incomprehensible. And in other cases there was just a knowledge that someone they loved had died, even if there was no reason to believe that this might happen at the time. These next two stories illustrate some of these strange occurrences. The first was sent to me by Danielle.

The Kiss

I was on my way home from work when I could have sworn that someone kissed me. I remember the time exactly because I was waiting for my train to arrive and it was ten minutes late, and I kept checking the clock. The time was 6.52 p.m.

I didn't get home until about 9.30 p.m., as there were so many delays on the trains. I was very tired and headed straight for the shower, and then I had something to eat. I didn't get to check my phone messages until almost eleven o'clock. When I did, I found out that my sister had died. I went into shock as last I heard my sister had moved down to London to get her degree. She'd died in a freak boating accident. She had been pulled out of the water alive and rushed to hospital but died at 6.50 p.m.

It was only a few days later as I was helping Mum with the funeral arrangements that I remembered what had happened to me – the kiss on the station platform. I believe it was my sister saying goodbye. I really believe that and I hope you find my story of interest.

And the second story was emailed to me by Misha.

Passing Through

They say that a mother has a telepathic link with her children, and when my son died earlier this year in a car accident I felt him. I heard him. I was driving to work and it was around seven in the evening. I was late for work and a bit anxious and angry because I was approaching a train crossing and the lights were flashing. I knew I had to stop, so I sat there fuming and waiting for the train to come. It seemed to take ages but then suddenly a blast of air hit my face full on. It was so strong I remember checking to see if my windows were open, but they were all closed. I checked my air conditioning and that was switched off too. I had no idea what had caused it and thought it might be somehow coming from outside, as I was first in the queue for the train crossing, but then I heard my son, Mica, talking to me. It wasn't like a normal conversation. I knew he wasn't in the car but I heard him inside my head – if that makes sense. He told me that I should not stress about being late and that he was just passing through and wanted to tell me he loved me.

I thought I was going nuts and wondered if I might be coming down with something. At that moment the train – it was a high-speed one – came rushing past. It was as the train was hurtling in front of me that I had this absolute certainty that something terrible had happened to Mica. I didn't know at the time that he had already passed over but I knew that something was very, very wrong. Do you think that the voice I heard and the gust of wind that blew around me was Mica on his way to heaven? His accident happened around 6.30 p.m. that same night.

Another gripping experience that can occur around the time of death is dreaming of a departed loved one. Numerous people have got in touch with me since the publication of my previous books to tell me about vivid and realistic dreams that they have had of departed loved ones. Dreams of the afterlife – or, as I prefer to call them, night visions – are a source of great comfort following the loss of a loved one, and in my mind they offer yet more proof that the afterlife is real; but, sadly, there just isn't time or space in this book to discuss them. I will, however, talk about them at length in my next book.

As we saw earlier, many scientists and psychologists suggest that parting visions and inexplicable feelings or experiences at the moment of death are the product of a grieving mind stretching for some kind of relief. While there is a thread of logic to these arguments, I've come to believe that such experiences are indeed messages of love from the other side. I believe this because, although the experiences are well reported, not all people who have lost a loved one or witnessed the moment of death have experienced them. Surely, if they were grief-induced experiences, wouldn't everyone experiencing intense grief have experienced them? In addition, the grief-induced explanation, or the explanation that such experiences are projections of an overactive imagination, do not explain away experiences where the recipient does not know that the person has died. I think there is more evidence to disprove such theories than prove them.

All the evidence suggests to me that deathbed visions are just what they reveal themselves to be to the people who experience them. They are proof that there is an afterlife and that, when our time comes, the spirits of loved ones and/or beings of light will be there to ease our transition from this life to the next. For the dying person, they are a source of great comfort and strength and they feel so real and reassuring that they can sometimes become a catalyst for physical change. This could be something as simple as a smile, colour rushing to the cheeks or the momentary return of lucidity and happiness and contentment. In my mind, such moments of clarity offer a preview of the spirit's eternity that is always there even in the most tired, ill and worn-out bodies.

In my books I often like to quote the words of William Blake, a poet with a strong belief in the existence of the afterlife. For Blake death was as natural and as simple as moving from one place to another. According to his wife, this strong belief sustained and comforted him in the days before his death and he was happier than she could have imagined. The philosopher Søren Kierkegaard also left this world with the absolute conviction that his life was not ending and he was starting a wonderful voyage. Speaking of the manner of Kierkegaard's death, his nephew is quoted as saying, 'Never have I seen a spirit break through the earthly husk and impart to it such glory.' The nephew then goes on to say that, after Kierkegaard said farewell to his family, he gave them 'a look the match of which I have never seen. It shone out from a sublime and blessed splendour that seemed to me to make the whole room light. Everything was concentrated in those eyes as the source of light and heartfelt love, the blissful dissolution of sadness, a penetrating clearness of mind, and a jesting smile.'

How I love that description, as it shows the delightfully happy state that Kierkegaard was in. So powerful was his belief in an afterlife that the prospect of death held absolutely no fear for him. This total absence of fear is a familiar theme in many stories I have read about people in their dying hours. Another theme is the effect that this absence of fear has on loved ones and family members struggling to cope with the prospect of losing those they care deeply about. Amy sent me this next story. She was present at the death of her mother and in the final hours she witnessed in her mother a joy, happiness and a glow of health and wholeness that not only eased her grief but removed any anxiety about death she previously had.

The Last Gift

I'd never seen someone die before. The doctors told me Mum only had days left to live and I should expect the worst. Little did I know that I would emerge from the experience expecting the best when it comes to death ...

Mum was in a great deal of pain in the months prior to her death and this distressed me more than the fact that I was going to lose her. She was on all sorts of medication and morphine to ease her suffering and there were days when I did long for her to pass over just so that she would be in peace and free of pain.

On the day she died I was sitting with her reading when I noticed that her deep and heavy breathing had quietened down to a gentle rhythm. I got up and, as I did, she opened her eyes and smiled and winked at me. It was so surprising I didn't know whether to laugh or cry. She couldn't sit up but her face looked radiant. Her lips were wet and her cheeks were rosy and her hair – which had previously looked dry and thin – was radiant and glossy, just as I remembered it when I was a child.

It was the most wonderful gift seeing her like this and we spent about thirty minutes talking and laughing and telling each other how much we loved each other. During that time Mum continued to sparkle and I will never forget this last gift she gave me. Instead of remembering her thin and pale and racked with pain, I have this wonderful memory of her glowing with health. After our chat Mum fell asleep and never woke up. In the moments before Mum's death she was never more alive to me than she had been for years and I truly believe after what I experienced that she is still alive somewhere and that dying is not the end of our journey.

I hope I will be filled with feelings of joy, peace and certainty like the people whose stories are in this chapter, but I know that I can't be certain of that. I may not be blessed with a vision of the afterlife when my time comes. I may not hear or see anything supernatural but this is not something I worry about as, for reasons I do not understand, not everyone experiences such lucidity; but, if this is the case, I know that I have no need to spend my final moments paralysed with anxiety and fear. As long as I hold onto my belief that the afterlife is for real, I can conquer any fear I might have about dying.

If you have never witnessed the end of life, or have been there but found the experience too unsettling and distressing, I urge you to read the stories in this chapter again. They all describe that treasured and sacrosanct moment when heaven touches earth and peace, love and comfort shine through. They all show that death can be beautiful and they are all powerful reminders that death is not stronger than love and that fear is a barrier to true understanding.

Yet, despite all this, it can be very hard not to think about death as something that is negative. The survival instinct is strong and most people tend to think about death as something that cannot happen to *us* or the people we love. But right now none of us has any idea how much time we have left of this earth – it could be decades, years, months, weeks, days or hours. We simply do not know.

Thinking about the certain prospect of our death from time to time is not a negative thing. Indeed, it can be an incredibly positive thing, as it can help us live our lives in a happier, more compassionate and enriching way.

There are, of course, some wise souls among us who already have this instinctive understanding of death. If you ever need a shot in the arm to believe in an afterlife, hear what young children have to say on the topic. They don't believe in death in the way that we do. I'll return to the subject of children seeing spirits later, but felt this was the best place for this next story, from Henry, because it can teach us adults so much about the reality of life and death.

Up There

I am a father of four children, but if you ask my two-and-a-half-year-old daughter Emma she will say that she has four brothers and sisters. I have told her over and over again that she has two sisters and one brother but she always shakes her head, laughs and says that she has two brothers. The first time it happened was when we took her to nursery for the first time. She was asked to draw a picture of her family. She drew me and Suzanne, my wife, and then she drew herself and her two sisters – Jade and Cordelia – and her brother, Jonathon and then, floating beside us, she drew

these signs from the world of spirit that have brought me comfort and feelings of strength and hope, but the stories I have read over the years about near-death experiences, deathbed visions and parting visions. Stories like those I have gathered together for you in this and the previous chapter.

Indeed, as I wrote both these chapters I could feel the tension inside me mounting up and on more than one occasion I had to stop and have a big cry. Simply writing the words 'I wasn't by her side when she died' was hard enough, but then something astonishing started to happen. As I added story after story to the chapters, those tears of pain and sadness gradually began to melt into tears of comfort and joy. A deep sensation of peace filled me, along with an awareness that I was finally learning a profound truth. I may not have been there physically for my mother, but these accounts, with their emphasis on the eternal power of love, have made it clear to me that I was with her every step of the way. And the reason for my conviction is the bond of love between my mother and me. Our love for each other was powerful enough to transcend the physical distance between us when she died. It was strong enough to be present with her and hold her hand when she crossed over. My mum wasn't alone when she died. I was with her in spirit, just as she is alive in spirit and with me now.

Writing this chapter has reminded and reassured me once again that heaven is real. It has taught me yet again that death is not the end but, to risk repeating myself, what I think or feel really, really doesn't matter. What matters here is what *you* think or feel and how reading this book is affecting you. Of course, you may still have doubts and find it all hard to swallow – and that is entirely understandable. All I am asking is for you to examine the evidence I'm presenting and reflect on whether it might help you to re-examine the priorities in your life in some way. It's a tired old cliché, but nobody on their deathbed ever says, 'I wish I'd spent more time at the office' and, as far as I know, all the phone calls to family and loved ones from the doomed planes involved in 9/11 were messages of love. As I always say, I am not here to convince you, just to present my case for the existence of an afterlife so you can come to your own conclusions and make your own decisions about what really matters in your life.

And, talking about presenting my case for the reality of heaven, if you were intrigued by deathbed visions, you'll be even more intrigued by the next chapter, because it contains stories sent to me by people who were not at the brink of death when they saw spirits.

Yes, the evidence is really mounting up now.

CHAPTER FOUR

Visitations from the Other Side

I have always thought of visitations as love letters from the infinite.

Lee Lawson

A visitation is a spontaneous encounter with the spirit of a departed loved one. If you can't help but think that the stories you've read so far could have physical or psychological explanations due to the shock, pain, grief and unresolved tensions that typically surround the immediate death of a loved one, then I would like to bring to your attention the accounts in this chapter. All the people here believe they actually saw or encountered, in an unmistakable way, the spirit of a departed loved one, but the visitation did not happen around the time of the loved one's death, but typically months, years or even decades later.

The stories here could perhaps be dismissed as tricks of the eyes and/or the mind. Eyes do indeed play tricks on us and the imagination can indeed distort our thinking, but let me get a few things straight right from the start. First of all, the people who sent me these stories assured me they were not under the influence of drugs, alcohol or medication – it was easy for them to identify what they were seeing – and neither were they psychologically disturbed in any way. They were perfectly ordinary people leading ordinary lives. Second, none of the people writing to me had any reason to make things up, and, in some cases prior to the visitation, they would have described themselves as nonbelievers who questioned the very existence of life after death. Third, although some were grieving the loss of a loved one at the time of the visitation, others were not even thinking of the deceased person at all and in all cases the visitation was spontaneous – there seemed to be no trigger. And last, but by no means least, everyone who contacted me swore that what they saw, heard and felt was real – they were not imagining it. I believe them.

Seeing spirits

This first cluster of stories comes from people who believe they actually saw departed loved ones and the spirits appeared to them in ways that were not elusive or shadowy but solid and genuine. In other words, the spirits looked concrete and real and, if the observers had not known that the people they saw were dead at the time of the visitations, the spirits could be mistaken for ordinary people. In addition, the spirits appeared healthy and happy regardless of how old and in what state of health their corporeal selves were when they died. Indeed, in many cases the departed loved ones looked more content in their spiritual form than when last alive in their physical form. There was a peace and tranquillity about them that they may not have exhibited in their human form, and this calm feeling impacted on the observer, who typically described the visitation as a healing and positive experience. Time and time again I have heard how seeing the spirit of a departed loved one helped the observer leave behind any painful recollections, unresolved tensions or feelings of guilt they may have had about losing someone who meant a lot to them.

This first story was sent to me by Sophie, and I think it illustrates perfectly the healing effect a full appearance by a departed loved one can bring.

Feet First

When I was fifteen I dropped out of school for a term because my father died. We had been very close and I cried for days, weeks and months afterwards. My father had been an atheist all his life and we gave him a humanist funeral according to his wishes. It was a beautiful and happy event that celebrated his life, but I went to pieces afterwards. I missed him so much and was not looking forward to anything. Mum tried to get me back on track with my school work but my head and heart weren't in it. I just drifted from one day to the next. The pain eased as weeks turned into months but it was always there ready to surface. I left school with five GCSEs and went to work in a coffee bar. It wasn't great and the work was dull, but it gave my life a routine and a structure and temporary relief from the pain of my loss. Grief is exhausting. It sucks the life out of you but having a job took my mind off things and I slowly began to recover. There were days when I felt so low, but then I would have a day when life didn't feel so bad any more. Progress was slow but I was on the way.

Then one evening I was getting some supplies from the café store cupboard and I accidentally locked myself in. I knocked on the door but the café was busy and noisy and I knew it would take a while before anyone would come looking for me. I resigned myself to waiting and sat down on the floor. The peace and quiet in the storeroom was refreshing after the hustle and bustle of work and I took my shoes off as my feet ached. I think it was the peace and quiet that got me going again and before long I was crying, as it was exactly a year and three days since my dad's death. We had had an anniversary but I didn't find it helpful, quite the opposite. It was then, as I was rubbing my sore feet, that I had the most sensational experience. I saw a pair of boots first – my dad's boots – and then I saw his legs appear and his body and his face. He was standing, or should I say floating, there right in front of me. I saw him. I really saw him. He held out his hand and I took it. It felt warm and alive and he helped me stand up. I opened my mouth to speak to him but at that moment the door opened and my boss came in. My dad had gone. I must have looked pretty spooked as my boss gave me the afternoon off – something he never does. I didn't tell him or anyone about what I had seen. This wasn't because I didn't think anyone would believe me, but because I wasn't ready to share – I wanted to keep this to myself for a while. It was my experience, if you know what I mean.

My mum and dad never pushed their atheist beliefs on me but I naturally was inclined to believe what they believed and my dad was always very passionate and stubborn in his belief. I worshipped Dad and assumed he had always got things right. I know different now. I did eventually tell my mum about seeing Dad's spirit and she didn't believe me, so that is why I decided to write to you. Dad was always such an opinionated and strong-willed man, it makes me smile to think how he would have reacted when he found out he was wrong all along about life after death. He would have been so shocked but it must be wonderful up there because he swallowed his pride and came back to let me know he hadn't died. I figure if Dad could do that for me it's time for me to have a rethink too. I still don't know what I want to do with my life and I'm still working in the coffee bar, but in the evenings I'm studying for some A levels. I don't want to drift any more.

After her dad appeared, Sophie felt at peace and was comforted by the certain knowledge that he was always by her side. Yes, it is possible to argue that her experience had a psychological explanation or perhaps even a physical one – as she did say she was exhausted by her grief – but, at the start of her story, Sophie points out clearly that she had never believed in life after death until her experience. In other words, she wasn't unconsciously seeking out the experience when it happened – quite the opposite, as she also says that she was on the road to recovery.

Julie sent me this intriguing story.

Clear as Day

My mother-in-law was diagnosed with pancreatic cancer in 2004. She became very ill in December that year and we all knew it wouldn't be long before she would pass away.

We got the phone call on the night of 26 December 2004 and were told the time she died. We went to see her that night to say goodbye. The next morning we heard about the Thailand tsunami and found out that it had hit at the exact same time my mother-in-law died. The day after her funeral I was sitting in my lounge room and saw clear as day two figures standing in my entranceway. One was my mother-in-law, and she was wearing her long black coat that she always wore in the winter. She was holding the hand of a young boy and he was wearing white shorts, no shirt, and he had bare feet. I thought I was imagining it but it was real. They were not there long, they walked in the direction of my hallway and then they were gone.

I really do believe that my mother-in-law was taking care of a young child that had died in the tsunami as she was so very close to my son and I know how much she loved him, so I think she helped another boy to find their way.

Rosemary sent me this brief but illuminating story.

Fleeting

My father died ten years ago and one evening I was turning into my drive when I saw my father as clear as day – I could even describe what he was wearing – just for a fleeting minute.

And Naelene sent me this story about a visitation from her departed husband.

Wide Awake

I am an elderly lady of seventy-seven years, and years ago, when my first husband Basil died, I believe I had an afterlife encounter. After Basil died I was very upset and one night I had a dream we were playing golf and he hit his ball into some trees, went to look for it and then disappeared. I couldn't find him any more and my crying woke me up. Then, when I was wide awake and lying on my side, I suddenly heard Basil cough, and I leaned over and smelled his familiar aftershave. Then I saw him. I actually saw him. I wasn't imagining it. He was dressed in black shorts and had no top on. He had long hair and sported a beard, which was unusual because he was a short-back-and-sides-haircut-and-clean-shaven man.

All of a sudden I felt him holding me and I could feel his warmth. I laughed as his beard scratched my face. Communicating, I now believe by thought, he said I should marry again but I said I only wanted him. With that he was gone, leaving me weeping, and I continued to cry for the rest of the night.

Although visitations can bring feelings of loss and sadness to the surface again at the same time, as Naelene's story shows, they can also bring soothing feelings of joy and reassurance that a departed loved one is still alive and loving us just as before – but in another dimension.

Christina sent me this next story. It is clear that catching a glimpse of her stillborn daughter Sarah in spirit brought her and her family a very real sense of peace and hope.

Still Alive

I have read a few of your books and find them hard to put down. I want to share with you an incredible experience I had after losing my daughter, Sarah, who was a stillborn.

My two daughters are a year apart. Madison is two years old. Sarah should be six months old. One day Madison was playing while I washed the dishes and she kept saying, 'Hello, little rabbit.' I asked, 'Where is the rabbit?' Madison pointed at the doorway. Then again, she said, 'Hello, little rabbit.' I asked where, and she pointed at the ceiling. I asked if I could say hello and Madison said no because she's gone. Then she smiled and said, 'Hello, back now. Mum, can I have some milk?' As I looked up to tell her yes, I saw a little girl run out of the room. The same features as Sarah had and would look if she were about two years old. I believe it was Sarah because I wrote in Sarah's record book that she was born in the Year of the Rabbit.

Another thing I noticed when reading visitation stories is that departed loved ones do seem to have knowledge of what is going on in the world they left behind. Sometimes in times of crisis they will visit to offer guidance, strength and courage. This was exactly what happened to Ron.

Lost and Found

My wife died when my girls – Lizzy and Stacey – were just heading into their teenage years. We had a hellish few years and I probably didn't handle things as well as I could. I took two months off work after the funeral and spent every moment with the girls. We were amazingly close at that time and I thought that this two-month period was all that they really needed. When the two months were over I plunged myself into work. I figured that I had two teenage daughters to support and what they wanted from their dad now more than anything was financial security. I thought that they were almost women and were handling the loss okay and moving forward with their lives but I got it very wrong. They were still very much children in need of guidance.

It was close to three years after my wife died that my daughter's school called me in to see them. Apparently Lizzy had been slipping behind in her work and being less than courteous to the staff there. There had been an incident of serious rudeness and she was given a warning and a three-day suspension. This was out of character but I figured everyone gets it wrong sometimes and Lizzy would not repeat her mistakes after this punishment. I was up to my ears in work and couldn't take any time off but, as she was a mature fifteen, I thought that she would be fine on her own at home.

Again, I got it wrong. When I came back from work to check on her at lunchtime she was nowhere to be seen. I was frantic with worry. I called her on her mobile but there was no answer. I drove to all her local haunts but she was not there either. I dropped into the local police office to ask for advice and they said that, as she had only been missing a few hours, they were not able to do anything yet. They tried to be positive, saying she would probably come home in the evening and the best place for me right now was to wait at home so I was there when she came back.

I went home and the afternoon passed in an agonisingly slow way. Stacey came home at five and when she found out her sister was missing she went hysterical and started swearing at me and saying it was my fault. I tried to talk to her but she just went to her room and slammed the door in my face. I felt such a complete and utter failure as a father and utterly helpless, as I had absolutely no idea whether to do what my instinct told me and go looking for Lizzy, or wait at home as the police had suggested.

It was then that I saw my wife sitting on the sofa in the living room. Time stood still. I closed my eyes and opened them again to make sure I wasn't dreaming. This was impossible. I walked towards her and she turned her head to look at me and smiled her knowing smile. She looked amazing. In the last few months of her life the cancer had really taken its toll but now she looked just like I remembered her when we first met. She was stunning. I asked her to help me but she shook her head and then smiled again – that reassuring smile she always used to give me when she trusted me to do something.

I was just about to ask for help again when I heard Stacey coming down the stairs. I turned around and when I looked back my wife had gone. Stacey came in and asked me if I was okay, as she had heard me shouting. As far as I remember I wasn't shouting. I was just begging my wife for help. Before I could reply Stacey came and gave me a huge hug and as she hugged me I suddenly had a brilliant idea. I had checked every single place except the only obvious place – the cemetery.

My suspicions were right and I did find Lizzy at the cemetery. She had taken a packed lunch and some work and sat there all afternoon. I'm convinced my wife appeared to guide me to Lizzy and also to remind me that even though my daughters were young adults they still missed their mother deeply and needed me there more than ever before. Time can heal but healing was going to be a slow process, and, even if they seemed okay, I needed to be there, really be there for them.

I have also read a number of compelling stories which show that departed loved ones don't want grief and feelings of loss to stop those they left behind from living life to the full. Coleen's story is a perfect example.

Wonderful Here

Mum died suddenly last year and it took me a long time to recover. She had been my rock. The first person I called for advice about anything. It had always just been the two of us and the world seemed very frightening without her. I was in my early twenties but inside I still felt very young and uncertain. I had a good job in a bank and Mum left me her flat and enough money to make sure I would be okay, so it wasn't about financial security: it was about *emotional* security. I found it hard to trust other people. As I said, it had always been just about me and Mum.

I did not realise it at the time, but the way I dealt with my fear was to retreat into my shell. I would go to work and then come straight back home. The more isolated I got the more I lost my appetite and before long I had gone down two dress sizes. I got a lot of compliments at work about my weight loss, so I kept on cutting down, and I also started exercising every day. At first the exercise gave me a huge lift. I felt strong and powerful but three years down the line my whole life was dominated by how little food I had eaten and how much I had exercised. I didn't think it at the time but I looked so unwell and bony, but this didn't bother me. I wanted to be thin – really thin. Finally, I had found something that I could do well.

And then, four years after my mum died, I had what I can only describe as a revelation. It was about five in the morning and I was doing my customary sit-ups in the living room when I saw my mum sitting at the kitchen table. She looked amazing. She told me that she was very happy in heaven and that she missed me a lot, but it wasn't my time to join her yet. She then said that they served the most wonderful food in heaven and the only thing that made her sad was that she couldn't eat it because I wasn't eating on earth. She asked me to please let her eat.

The vision ended abruptly when my exercise alarm went off to signal for me to do star jumps. I switched it off and felt ravenous hunger for the first time in years. In honour of my mum, though, I didn't stuff myself with any food I could get my hands on. I showered, got dressed and went and had breakfast in style at a hotel nearby. It tasted so good and, as I ate, I imagined my mum in heaven eating too. This was to be the first of many treats, and within a few months I was back to my normal weight. I can, hand on heart, say that my anorexia has been cured. There's a lot of talk online about miracle cures for anorexia and I wonder what people would think if I told them about mine!

Coleen's mother didn't want Coleen to destroy her life any more. She wanted her to know that she was happy in her new spiritual body and to reassure her that she hadn't gone away. This next story goes one step further. Not only did Mark see and talk to his father: he felt his father hug him.

One Moment

My dad died when I was fourteen. We had had such a great relationship and it was a terrible blow. We had always had this running joke about who was the tougher guy, and until his death (from a road accident) he was always the tougher one. He could easily beat me in play fights because I was obviously smaller and had weaker muscles.

After I turned sixteen I had the most life-changing experience, and to this day (I'm fifty-three now) I can remember it in minute detail. I woke up one morning and it was getting colder as winter was drawing in. I rummaged in my cupboard and got a pair of old winter trousers out, but when I put them on they were way too small. I must have had a huge growth spurt. It was then that I clearly heard the voice of my dad saying that I could probably beat him up now. I wasn't at all frightened and when I turned around there was my dad. He was laughing and saying how proud he was of me, and then he gave me this enormous bear hug. It was the most comforting hug I have ever had and filled me with feelings of hope, strength and positivity. I shall never forget how it felt. It was real.

I heard Mum shout at me from downstairs that breakfast was ready and at that moment my dad vanished. One moment he was there and the next he had gone. He may have been gone physically but the memory of that hug has stayed with me for ever.

I love Mark's story, as it describes a visit from a departed loved one in such a warm and real way. Mark knows that what he experienced was not a figment of his imagination and I believe every word he says. His story again offers confirmation that there is an afterlife.

Fleeting glimpses

Sometimes people will recognise an incomplete rather than a full appearance from a departed loved one. Such accounts describe seeing a departed loved one appear as a bright light or just seeing part of their body – typically head and shoulders – or perhaps seeing the whole body as a kind of vague shadow or mist. Even though the experience is less solid than a full experience, it has the same effect: it brings great solace to the observer.

This next story, from Mandy, describes the appearance of a departed loved one as an intense, bright light.

Vivid

Our beloved daughter Charlotte passed away eighteen weeks ago, due to an accidental overdose of paracetamol. Last week, early in the morning, her father jumped up wide awake saying he could see something. I woke up too and could see a very vivid light similar to the colour of flames. It just faded away. In the morning our other daughter said she had a dream about Charlotte and then Charlotte's friend emailed me and explained she too had dreamt about Charlotte. Could this be coincidence, or was it Charlotte letting us know she is safe?

I wrote back to Mandy to tell her I believed the flamelike light she saw was a sign from Charlotte. This is Denise's story.

Saying Goodbye

My husband and I delayed our honeymoon to save for the trip of a lifetime to South Africa. Two days before we were due to depart my beloved grandfather passed away. I wanted to cancel the trip but my grandmother insisted we go ahead. I was fourteen weeks pregnant at the time but we were keeping it quiet. The night before we left, about 3.30 a.m., I was awoken by the most vivid orange light at the end of the bed. I could feel heat and intensity, as it travelled towards me. It encircled my womb and lingered for a couple of seconds and then slowly left. My husband bolted up in the bed, shouting that there was something in the room, all set to defend me from an intruder. I managed to calm him down by telling him that it was only Granddad in spirit coming to say goodbye. The following morning he had no recollection of what happened. I remembered everything, though, and had a lovely sense of ease as I felt the connection so intensely, and my pregnancy progressed really well.

Katia wrote from Italy to tell me about her experience.

Clear

Forty days ago I lost my mother unexpectedly, without even time to say goodbye. I was pregnant and, one week after this loss, I was not able to complete my pregnancy. It has been the worst period of my life, in which the loss of my mother overcame the loss of my daughter.

One night while I slept, I clearly heard a female voice calling me by name once. I opened my eyes and I saw in front of me, reflected clearly on the wall, a rectangular horizontal light about thirty centimetres long. At that moment I realised that light was not coming from anywhere and I also heard my six-year-old daughter talking as she slept in her room. I believe that light was my mother.

It is often the case in stories about the appearance of the spirit of a departed loved one in the form of a bright light that it is night-time when the experience occurs and the bright light is the only source of light to fill the room. In this next account Paula describes how she saw the face of her husband in a bright light and how the experience gave her the will to live again.

Smashed

I didn't want to live after my Wayne died. But I believe he wants me to live. I will tell you why. One night I was reaching for yet another bottle of wine to blot out the pain when I was dazzled by this bright light, and in that light clearly saw my Wayne's face appear in front of me. I had had a drink but not that much. I wasn't drunk, I promise you. I could see Wayne smiling and winking at me. It freaked me out a bit and I dropped the bottle I had reached for and smashed it. I haven't had a drop to drink since. I think my Wayne came back to tell me to take better care of myself and our three-year-old son. He doesn't need a drunk for a mother. He needs a mother.

Another category of visual afterlife experiences is those that involve living pictures, photographs or reflections of departed loved looking through an illuminated window or glass from their dimension to ours – if that makes sense. In contrast to appearances that have a realistic feel about them, these visitations have an otherworldly feel. These visions can occur with the eyes open or shut. Those that occur with the eyes open are typically compared to watching a movie or projection or a hologram, and those that occur with the eyes closed are seen as a vivid image on the surface of your eyes.

Such visions are a rare but fascinating form of after-death communication. They are often described as *creating a light of their own*, and those who have the vision often say that they are instinctively aware that what they are watching is from the world of spirit – regardless of whether or not they believed in the world of spirit prior to the experience. Sometimes the vision is accompanied by telepathic messages. This next story was sent to me from Brazil. Once again, we see how such experiences offer the certain knowledge that a loved one has entered a happier, more content life. In this case, it is Laila's story of her mother, and the reassurance that her pain and suffering were over.

Finados

Your book touched me mainly because of a coincidence: today is my mom's birthday, when she would be eighty-five years old (she died four years ago).

I can't imagine what you know about my country, but,

since it's a new one, it's a miscellany of cultures of many countries around the world and, of course, Native Indians – the few that still exist. Anyway, it means that I'm influenced by a great sort of beliefs, though I'm not a religious person. I told you this to introduce a vision that I had after my mom died. She'd been in a coma for almost ten days, and I was eager to see her smiling again, or at least squeezing my hand on the hospital bed. That never happened but on 2 November 2007, nine days after she died, I decided to go to a Catholic Mass of Deceased (this day here is called Finados, in honour to dead people) in a small church near my house. I'd never been there, and during the service I was looking at the altar and had a vision of my mom. She was floating there in midair looking beautiful, with a great smile and a light expression, waving goodbye to me. Since then I began to think she was happy, and have had various dreams about her, usually in ordinary family reunions. One more detail: my mom's name was Linda, a word that means, in Portuguese, beautiful.

Internal images appear suddenly in a person's mind. They typically occur with the eyes closed, but can also occur with the eyes open. The person knows that the image is happening in their mind and not outside in the physical world, but they also know instinctively that the image was not created within their mind but somehow projected there from another dimension. Paul's experience happened when his eyes were closed and he was just about to fall asleep.

Surreal

I heard my cat jump off my bed and this gave me a start. I opened my eyes and closed them and was drifting off nicely to sleep when I saw a picture of my brother Steven. He had been dead sixteen years but I saw him. I couldn't hear what he was saying but he was moving his arms and talking to me and seemed really happy. I opened my eyes and couldn't see him, but then I closed them and he was back. It was very surreal and went on for about half an hour.

The only way I can describe it is like looking at a movie on the inside of your eyelids. It didn't frighten me – quite the contrary. I would love it to happen again but it never has. My brother committed suicide and I have often wondered about him and this experience – whatever it was (perhaps you could enlighten me, Theresa?) has really helped me come to terms with what he did.

From all that I have read or studied, it does not seem to matter whether a vision is seen with eyes open or closed, or even whether it appears solid and real or elusive and transparent, because in all cases the impact on the observer is exactly the same. The observer emerges from the experience with the certain knowledge that their loved one is alive and happy in spirit and that life will go on after the corporeal body dies.

Sprits on film

From a sceptic's point of view, a huge problem with visitation stories is that because the experience typically happens when a person is alone there is never any record apart from the word of the observer. The word of an honest person is good enough for me. I have no reason to doubt anyone who writes to me, especially as many of these people write to me in the humblest of fashions, expressing shock and surprise that something like this actually happened to them. They often say that they themselves find it hard to believe it happened – but happen it did. They were not imagining it. In most cases, the experience is so unexpected and extraordinary that few have the presence of mind or the equipment on hand to try to record it, but from time to time I do get stories sent to me from people who believe they have been able to create a permanent record on camera.

Whenever I am sent photographs of what looks like a spirit I'm typically asked whether the image is genuine, as these days faking photographs is a very easy thing to do. In many cases the photo was taken by someone who had no interest or even knowledge of the departed loved one. In other words, there is no agenda. It wasn't their intention to capture an image, it just happened, and they were just as shocked as everyone to see it. Over the years, I've received pictures of shadowy human forms, heads and shoulders of departed loved ones posing behind a family photograph or at a family gathering and photographs of misty faces in globes of light. My first reaction when I view these kinds of photographs is excitement, but then frustration, because I can't reply and tell the person who has sent the photo to me that I am 100 per cent convinced the images are not caused by flaws in the film or developing, or by fog or specks of dust on the camera, or by light reflected from the lens or simply by random light patterns that can be created in natural settings or shadows. The pictures may look over-whelmingly real and convincing but I can't ever say for sure. What I do give the sender, though, is information gathered from experts in spirit photography, like those from the Ghost Research Society (GRS) of Illinois which contains a fascinating collection of spirit photographs that have been carefully analysed in minute detail by photographic expects and scientists.According to experts in spirit photograpy, about ninety out of every hundred spirit photographs they receive can be explained naturally, and that leaves about ten that can't. About eight of these remaining ten turn out to be photos of shadows and/or blocks of light that are very hard to explain, so that leaves a very rare two out of every one hundred that appear to defy all natural and logical explanations, and this rare 2 per cent could be paranormal. Having given this information to the person who sent me the photograph, and possible addresses they may wish to send the photograph to for analysis, I then typically tell them that, if they are 100 per cent convinced there was no possibility of a natural or logical explanation, they could – and I stress the word *could* here – have something very rare indeed, and that is solid, tangible evidence or proof of an afterlife.

Here is Martin's story.

Graduation

When I was seventeen and graduating from school something remarkable happened. A few weeks before my graduation I was visiting my granddad and asked him to my mum and dad's house the night of my graduation, as we were having a little party. He said yes, he would come. I was delighted, as normally my family would go to Granddad's house. So for my granddad to say he would come meant a lot, as we were very close. Sadly, though, he passed away ten days before my graduation.

My granddad dying took a lot out of me, as I loved him very much. My mum and dad still went ahead with a little party the night of my graduation and a lot of my friends and some other family members came. My dad took a lot of photos and he took one of me and my girlfriend at the time. When we got them developed, there next to me on my shoulder was an image of my granddad. It was incredible and meant the world to me. My granddad came to my graduation.

Martin is convinced that his grandfather's image has been caught on film – and who are we to disagree? I love reading stories like his and seeing the evidence for myself, but it is important to stress that this kind of solid proof – proof that could very well defy all rational explanation – is exceedingly rare. Less rare, however, are photos of mysterious globes of light called *orbs*.

Orbs caught on film are thought by many people to indicate

the presence of a spirit. These balls of hazy light are never visible to the human eye when the photograph is taken but they will appear on a photograph and are typically very hard to explain. I can't include copies of the photos in this book because it is non-illustrated, but here is a selection of the kinds of letters I am often sent concerning them, to give you an idea.

Please see the attached photo of my daughter Lily, in many pictures of her appear two white orbs (always two). What do you think about this and do you know where I can get the photo analysed to rule out dust particles etc. I know it can't be dust as it's too coincidental how there's always two in her pictures.

Jenna

I sent a copy of the angel orb to my brother who is a pro photographer and he says it is caused by the flash on the camera, but I have taken hundreds of photos with this camera and this has never happened before. I think your explanation is the right one; when I study the enlarged photo of the orb I can see a face the eyes and mouth are facing right and looking slightly down; I believe this is an angel and I get a great feeling of peace every time I look at it.

Best regards
James

Just wanted to let you know that my friend has a pair of night vision goggles and you can actually see orbs flying about! It is the most amazing thing. The same friend came to mine the other day to try and get some orb photos. Well, he got one near to my mum's chair and one floating above the side of the bed she slept on! I was thrilled.

Paul

Last weekend my friends and I went for a walk in the country. My friend had just bought a new digital camera with Christmas money he had received and spent most of the walk taking pictures. When we got home we discovered some orbs in the photos (I have attached some of them – truly wonderful). That evening I was in bed reading your book – How to See Your Angels *– and I turned the page and saw right in front of me a section on orbs. I was delighted. I read all about orbs and everything just seemed to fit into place. This has happened to me often. I read every evening in bed before I go to sleep and it seems that every spiritual subject/theory/idea that is currently occupying my mind turns up in black and white in front of me and always at the right time. I find it truly amazing to think about spiritual things and then have them clarified or confirmed in black and white. It makes it so much more powerful.*

Carol

Just read your book How to See Your Angels *and found it fascinating. I was drawn to your book and glad I was as I really enjoyed it. I constantly have synchronicities and know I am guided and being protected every day. I just thought I'd send you the attached picture as you say you love to see orb photos sent to you; I get a lot of orb pictures and like you believe they are something more than photo malfunctions. I'd love to see what you make of the attached.*

Love and Blessings
Christina

I will send the story and the CD of all the orbs we have photographed so far to your publisher. As we live in the sticks here in Italy we are only on the old-fashioned dial-up connection and that makes it very difficult and slow to send photos, so it is better to mail the CD etc to you. Terri

Love and Light
Terri

PS. We started knocking out the chimney in the sitting room yesterday and captured orbs immediately in a room where they had never been before! One orb was on my husband's head as he was knocking out the bricks and the other orbs in the chimney cavity. It appears that as soon as we make our intention to do something to a particular part of the house the orbs appear. I will type up our story and mail it and CD to Simon & Schuster in the next couple of weeks.

Last night, as usual, I was reading about matters spiritual before I went to bed and was astonished to find out how frequently the manifestation of Celestial Beings in pictures is happening! Since you mentioned the desire to receive copies of orbs, I want to share a gift I received last year. We were at the Fall, where we deposited the ashes of my oldest daughter, she passed away the year before. Our family got together to pray. The place in itself transmits Peace and a Positive Energy. Many cameras were used to take pictures. I was blessed to have the orbs in my Camera. Hope you enjoy them.

Cleia

In every case the orb is unseen when the photograph is taken and shows up only when the film is developed. If you want to get a sense of just how many people are capturing orbs on film and how much interest there is today in orbs as an indication of the presence of spirit, just type in 'spirit orbs' or 'ghost orbs' on an Internet search engine and you will be amazed at the thousands of hits you get. There are sites from every corner of the globe packed with photographs, theories, witness statements and suggestions.

Scientists argue that orbs are caused by fraud or tricks of the light, lens flare, flaws in the film or water spots, and offer all kinds of other logical explanations, and I can't deny that in the majority of photographs this may very well be the case. However, when all possible explanations are exhausted I would simply like to say that if all orbs can be explained by technical flaws there must be a heck of lot of cameras in circulation that haven't been checked properly by their manufacturers (which seems highly unlikely to me in such a technologically advanced, competitive marketplace), judging by the vast numbers of orb photos posted on the Internet. Also orbs don't necessarily tend to be captured in places you would suspect them to be captured – for example, cemeteries – but at birthday parties or family get-togethers. In my opinion, when an image appears on film that appears to defy rational explanation the possibility that it *could be* paranormal should be considered, alongside all other explanations. I emphasise the words 'could be' here because they are such powerful words. It is a shame that sceptics don't include them more often in their vocabulary!

Reaching out

A large number of visitation stories don't involve visions of departed loved ones as such but they are still classed as visitation experiences because, although the person involved did not actually see a spirit, they believe they were touched, hugged, kissed or spoken to by a loved one in spirit. This next story, sent to me by Nicola, has a special place in my heart.

Invisible Kisses

My mother always told me that she didn't want me to see her body after she had died. She wanted me to remember her alive and vibrant, so when the doctor asked if I wanted to say one last goodbye I said no.

A day before the funeral my aunt and uncle asked the same question and once again I said no. They pressured me, saying that even though she had lost a lot of weight she looked peaceful, but I remembered what my mum had told me. I was pressured again by my husband, who told me that seeing my mum would be a healing process, but I had made my mind up. Everyone said I would regret my decision one day.

About an hour before the funeral I went to my bedroom to gather my thoughts. Tears welled up in my eyes. I thought of my mother lying cold and motionless in her coffin. Perhaps I should have given her one last kiss. Perhaps everyone was right and I needed the closure. At that moment I felt a refreshing breeze on my face. The breeze was so strong it wiped some of my tears away. My bedroom door was closed and there were no windows open. I knew it was my mother.

During the funeral I focused on the happy times Mum and I had shared and as I said my last goodbyes I felt invisible lips kiss my cheeks on both sides. I closed my eyes and saw an image of my mum smiling and dancing, just as she wanted me to remember her. I knew then that I had made the right decision. From now on, whenever I thought of her she would always be dancing and smiling by my side.

Nicola was thinking intensely about her mum when the experience happened, but this was not the case for Mary, who sent me this story.

Downtime

I was having a really stressful day at work and things got worse when I could feel myself coming down with a sore throat and a cold too. It was exams week at school and just impossible for me to take any time off, so I soldiered on as best I could. Things came to a head at lunchtime, when I was absolutely shattered. There was just no time to eat or even sit down, as so much was going on. I wondered how I would survive the day without at least a sit-down and as I was wondering this I felt my neck and shoulders being massaged gently, just like my first husband used to do.

My first husband had passed over eleven years previously from cancer and it broke my heart at the time, but eventually I found the strength to carry on with my life and five years ago I remarried. At the time a part of me felt like I had betrayed my first husband by remarrying, but I knew he would have wanted me to be happy. Feeling his loving touch again totally energised me and I found the energy from somewhere to keep going. It stopped me feeling like I was going down with something too. As I said, it totally energised me. I hope you find my story interesting. It was a really extraordinary experience for me.

Experiences involving the invisible physical touch of a deceased loved one are not a very common type of after-death communication. I do get a number of stories like this but not as many as other types of communication, and perhaps this could be because the experience is often very subtle and easily dismissed or mistaken for something else. For example, the experience may involve feeling a light tap on the shoulder, a brush on the cheek, a gentle kiss, an arm on the shoulder or even a hug.

Alongside experiences that involve touch, we come to experiences that involve auditory communication from the world of spirit. This is probably the part of this chapter that I was most apprehensive about writing, because one of my missions when writing about the afterlife is to show that spirit encounters happen every day to ordinary people. However, every time I give interviews and mention hearing the voices of departed loved ones, I am aware that many people think this sounds a little mad or crazy. I sincerely hope that the stories that follow will make it clear once and for all that hearing spirits has nothing to do with madness and everything to do with communication and guidance from the other side.

In Chapter One, you may recall, I mentioned how I once heard the clear voice of my mother in spirit urging me to take the right path and head in another direction. That spirit-inspired change of direction saved my life because, if I had turned left as I had intended when I set out on my journey, I would almost certainly have been involved in an accident that claimed three lives. I also told you about hearing the voice of one of these victims the very night of the accident and how that voice told me her name was Jane and she was okay. I did not find out the names of the accident victims until the following day. Yes, I have heard voices from the world of spirit and although I may be a little odd at times – aren't we all? – I'm not insane. I have got my wits about me. And I have had countless letters and emails from people who have experienced something similar. As far as I know none of these people are insane either. Like me, they were ordinary people going about their daily lives when something extraordinary happened to change their lives for ever. This is what happened to Sylvia.

Perfectly Natural

I have had an experience you may find interesting but first let me explain a little about myself. I worry a lot about things and have done for years. My husband died on the 22 December, 2002 and about three or four years ago I had gone to bed and woke to see him standing at the side of the bed. He looked perfectly natural and normal. The ensuing 'conversation' may seem strange but it was the way we were to each other. He asked me what I was worried about. I had recently adopted a dog who was not yet house-trained and I was worried that she might need to go out. My husband told me that the dog was awake now. I asked him why he didn't take her out and he looked shocked and told me it was three-thirty in the morning. I looked at my watch and that was the time. When I looked up again my husband had gone.

Theresa, the conversation felt perfectly natural to me in every way. It was just the way we were together when he was alive. I can't explain what it was but it was the most wonderful experience and I often feel that my husband is close by.

Scientists have been quick to dismiss such stories as the brain recollecting the familiar voice of a loved one, but this does not explain away stories where the departed person offers information the recipient did not know – as was the case for me when I heard the voice of Jane and she told me she had a child. Then there are stories, like this one below from Sasha, where a deceased loved one issues a clear warning.

Little One

I was doing the washing up and feeling very sleepy as my ten-month-old daughter had kept me up all night, when I clearly heard my mum's voice. She called my name and told me to check on my 'little one'. Mum always used to call my sister's children little ones but sadly she never got to see or hold my Tegan, as she died two years before Tegan was born. I thought I was hearing things, so I carried on washing up, but then I clearly heard Mum again tell me to go upstairs and check on Tegan. It freaked me out this time and I ran around the house downstairs to see if anyone was there. Then I went upstairs and I am so glad I did, because I'd forgotten to pull up the safety rail on Tegan's cot.

Mercifully, there was no harm done, as Tegan was fast asleep, but I shudder to think what might have happened if she had woken up, because she was a real wriggler and would almost certainly have fallen out. I don't know how I could have forgotten to pull up the rail, but I was feeling exhausted at the time. I think Mum came back to warn me and let me know that she had seen her grand-daughter.

Sometimes the voice will sound as if it were from an external source. The voice is heard as if it were a normal voice, as was the case for Sasha above, but on other occasions it will be internal – a kind of telepathy or mental communication – as was the case for Denise, who contributed a story earlier (see 'Saying Goodbye') and has another experience to share here.

Hearing Red

The mother of a close male friend passed away very suddenly, while I was away on holiday. I work as a massage therapist and invited my friend in for a treatment on my return.

At the end of the session, it was like a female voice whispered inside my ear to tell my friend that she liked the red. The message meant nothing to me and I tried to block it out. The voice persisted and encouraged me to pass the message on to my friend, lying on my treatment table. Eventually – and, I must admit, feeling a little embarrassed – I relayed the message to my friend. Instantly he became very emotional but, smiling, explained that his sister was buying a new car and couldn't decide between a grey or red one! He was convinced his mother was trying to get through from the other side.

I now work with cancer patients through massage and reflexology. It is such an honour to work in palliative care to help people on their journey. I give your books to people who are afraid, and they do help ease their burden, and open up.

As is often the case with stories like this, Denise heard a voice when she least expected it. Indeed, this 'least expected' theme is one that runs through many supernatural experiences. It seems that trying too hard to connect to the other side has the opposite effect. That may well explain why a lot of auditory experiences happen when people are driving, walking, doing chores and other similar repetitive activities or when they are in that twilight stage just before falling asleep or waking up. They are in a relaxed, almost meditative state and it seems that at such times people may be more open to those kinds of experiences.

We all have thoughts and voices rattling through our heads all the time, and another question I am often asked is how it is possible to know the difference between our own thoughts and communication from the world of spirit. Although this can never be an exact science, there are ways to know if the experience is supernatural. First of all, auditory communication from the world of spirit is typically short and to the point, like a telegram or text message. It is rare for the communication to last more than a dozen or so words. The voice will also be instantly recognisable and sound exactly as the deceased person did when they were alive. It will be calm, clear and nonthreatening. It will also be positive and uplifting and fill you with a sense of certainty and comfort. If the voice you hear makes you feel afraid, inferior or uncertain in any way, it is negative self-talk and not heaven speaking.

As well as sight, sound and touch, scent has been a major theme of a fair number of visitation stories I've been sent. Typically, the scent is one that is instantly associated with the departed loved one – for example, a familiar perfume or aftershave or brand of food or tobacco – but the scent may also resemble freshly cut flowers. In either case the person who experiences it knows that the source is supernatural because there is no other explanation.

Here is Emma's story about her friend Marcus.

Only Me

I lost my friend Marcus six years ago next month. He died three years after his accident. Recently I have been getting a smell of cigarettes lately and no one in our house smokes. There is only my daughter and myself and she never smells it. It's only me that can smell it. I just got a whiff just now as I'm typing to you. It doesn't scare me or bother me as I think it could be my friend Marcus coming to check on me and say Hi. Marcus would have been forty in June.

Most cases of after-death communication involving scent occur days, weeks, months or sometimes years after the death of a loved one. Amber's story is unusual in that she had the experience on the anniversary of her brother's death.

Forget Me Not

My brother was a handyman and always smelt of fresh paint – even when he wasn't working. Last week I was at home tidying up when I suddenly smelt fresh paint. My children were in the room at the time doing their homework and I asked them if they could smell it, but they couldn't. I didn't think much of it, but then, as I was getting ready for bed that evening, there it was again. I asked my husband if he could smell it but he couldn't. By now it was really making me think of my brother. I started to get emotional. I got even more emotional when my husband reminded me it was exactly seven years ago today that my brother had died. How could I have forgotten that? I felt so ashamed. It wasn't because I had forgotten him. He was always in my heart. For some reason – and it's unlike me – I had just got my days muddled up.

Perhaps the most common form of visitation is that which involves sensing or feeling the presence of a deceased loved one. Of course, this isn't as dramatic or as spectacular to report as an actual vision, and sceptics would dismiss it as not tangible, but, again, to the person involved it feels remarkable. They can't explain how or why but they just know that their loved one is with them in the same place. They know that he or she is close by and when they arrive and when they leave. They know because they can feel their presence.

This next story, from Pam, shows again that nothing can stand in the way of an expression of love from a departed family member or friend. The power of the heart is always greater than the power of death.

Feeling in My Heart

While I was preparing my dad's memorial tribute, I felt this lovely warm almost embracing feeling in my heart; I am almost certain my dad's spirit was walking in the garden. I could sense it. Also I could hear what sounded like lots of voices talking but I could not understand what they were saying. My heart was filled with happiness and made tears come to my eyes, I am sure this was spiritual energy.

Tina sent me this email.

Unc

The event occurred when we attended the funeral of my husband's uncle, referred to by everyone as Unc. He was not exceptionally close to my husband but my husband and his siblings all had a mutual respect for Unc.

Unc had been ill with liver cancer and he had a graveside funeral service only. At the time I was about three months pregnant with our first child. As we were standing near the graveside I stood back just slightly to let other family members be together. I'm not sure exactly when it occurred but all of a sudden there was something I can only describe as electricity and almost sparkly bits in the air. I could actually feel the electricity-type sensation, it made my skin prickle. I remember it made me smile like Unc was actually present there, and I looked around to see if anyone else could feel this weird sensation, but everyone else was bowed in prayer. It passed almost as quickly as it had started, but it felt really peaceful to me.

I never told my husband, or anyone, for that matter, of the event until some months later. Somehow it came up in conversation and I thought my husband would just laugh at me and tell me I imagined it but he didn't. I swore him to secrecy not to tell anyone but of course a while later he mentioned it to his mum. His mum said to me, 'That's okay, Tina, I feel Uncle Ray in the house all the time. Floorboards creak in the passage near the master bedroom and a presence can be felt in the house.' It turns out that the house that my in-laws lived in and my husband lived in during part of his childhood was built by Unc.

Alex also talks about sensations of peace and love following the death of loved ones.

At Peace

In your book, you asked your readers to share with you if they have received signs from the departed loved ones, and I felt compelled to share with you my experience and my mom's.

I was sixteen when my paternal grandma passed away. She lived with us and I had the privilege of having her loving presence every day throughout my growing years. She had a stroke one day and was hospitalised for a few weeks. She was in and out of consciousness. I took turns with my aunt to take care of her and one day she was very alert, talking to us and telling us how good we are, thanking our neighbour, who is a nurse who also came to see how she was doing, and then the next day she slipped into coma. The doctors told us to bring her home as she was slowly slipping away and there was nothing much they could do for her.

Two weeks later my grandma passed on. I was in school at that time and in a very noisy class. Suddenly there was this overwhelming silence and a sense of lightness and peace came unto me. I was drawn to this butterfly that was flying about in front of me. Somehow I knew it was my grandma, and that she has passed on. Half an hour later when my brother came to pick me up from school, he told me the bad news and I just cried.

About a week after her passing, I was crying in bed and missing her terribly, wondering how she was, if her soul was at peace, when suddenly I heard whispering in my ear I could not understand what was said, but I smiled, felt comforted, happy and at peace that I drifted off to sleep soon after.

My mom experienced something similar when her mother passed away. She was at the cemetery, wondering about her mother, whether they did right with the funeral rites. It was raining heavily when suddenly the rain stopped and a gust of wind rushed past her and the voices of her siblings faded away. She felt enveloped in happiness and peace and felt so lightweight as if she was floating and then she heard a voice whispering in her ear, 'She's at peace.' My mom never doubted after that if my maternal grandma was happy and at peace in the afterlife.

Another experience was very recent. It was from my best friend who died in a car crash five years ago. Another mutual best friend (there were always three of us very close to each other all the time, like sisters) and I continued to visit her parents and sisters on festive occasions like we used to do since we were teenagers. One day on the way to my departed friend's house, suddenly I felt so light, happy and peaceful, and particularly happy that we were going to visit her family, and I felt she was right there beside me. And I just knew that she wanted to tell me that she was happy that we still remembered her family and we still visited them on festive occasions even though she has passed on.

Jane's story is similar in that it features feelings of great comfort but different in that it does not involve the death of a family member or loved one.

Thank You

Only ten days ago, on my way to work, I was unfortunate enough to be at the scene of a car crash, just a couple of moments after it had happened. As a nurse, I felt I should stop to see if I could help. The motorcyclist who I knelt down to assess had clearly died, but I knew I had to make an attempt to save him, so started CPR [cardiopulmonary resuscitation] at the scene. However, it was no use and he was pronounced dead some time later when he was on the way to hospital in the ambulance.

This experience traumatised me. I was tormented by thoughts that I could have done more to help him. Some four days later, on the Friday night, I was again unable to sleep for thinking about him. I had been drinking, and began to cry for him and his family. After about five minutes of bitter sobbing, I felt myself engulfed in a comforting warm glow, and suddenly felt a sense of calm and peace wash over me, and I felt humbled. I know without a shadow of a doubt that it was him come to tell me it's okay, that he knows I tried my best, and to be at peace.

After this event happened, I know that heaven exists – he helped me in my bleakest moment of despair, just as I had helped him.

Do bear in mind that none of the people who sensed the presence of a spirit in the stories above described themselves as mediums or psychics. They were ordinary people, like you and me, who for a brief moment in time felt the closeness of heaven.

Most of the stories in this chapter were chosen because they showcase one particular type of after-death communication – for example, an encounter involving scent or one where voices are heard – but it is important to point out that in many cases the visitation will involve more than one type of communication. For instance, the person may sense a presence, hear a voice and recognise a familiar scent at the same time, or they may see their departed loved one in a vision and feel a comforting arm around their shoulder as well. Heather's story below is fascinating, as she experienced her visitation through a number of different senses.

Identical

I have had so many lovely experiences which I told my identical twin sister Hazel about. She believed in me but told me not to say anything to anybody in case they thought I might be going mad again. We were very, very close and felt we had a special connection; we were identical in looks but were mirror-image twins. We belonged to the Twin Research at St Thomas Hospital. Hazel and I used to love going to London for the day. All the hustle and bustle in London fascinated us, as we were proper country bumpkins. Sadly, Hazel was diagnosed with cancer in the chest and lung in 2008. She wanted to come and live with me for the last few weeks before she passed over. Although she was very weak we spent the last time she had left reflecting our lives together.

The reason I'm writing this letter to you is that out of all my experiences the most memorable I have is of Hazel. One afternoon in 2011 I was resting in my lounge feeling quite sad and still missing Hazel very much and wished she was still with me. Then all of a sudden I heard my name, Heather, being called in a very soft whisper. Then my heart felt very warm as though it was being massaged, and then all the sadness was being drawn out of me. I felt a very faint touch on my hand and a gentle squeeze on my arm. I just sat there for a while having this wonderful sensation of calmness and disbelief of what had just happened. I had actually heard my name, Heather. I felt so much love within me.

The next day I noticed a small brown mole on my hand just where I had been touched the day before. That made me realise it must have been Hazel that came to me because Hazel had exactly the same mole but on the opposite hand but in the same place. I often used to say to her she must get it checked as it could be cancerous. She had assured me it was okay. It had been checked a few years ago. Whenever I feel low and miss her I just have to look at my hand and see the mole and think back to that wonderful afternoon.

With Love, Heather

PS: We were born in two separate years, I ten minutes to midnight on 31st Dec and Hazel ten minutes after on 1st Jan.

I have so many more visitation stories I could have included here but space dictates that it is time to move on now. I hope, though, that the stories I did manage to include in this chapter have shown you that all these experiences – whether they involve sight, touch, sound, sense, smell or a combination of any or all of these – are extremely powerful occurrences that leave the person involved convinced that the afterlife is a reality, or at the very least an intriguing possibility.

Something extraordinary

It is wonderful that so many people continue to write to me and generously share their experiences, but sad that many still feel the need to justify themselves or state that they aren't crazy. I've lost count of the number of times people begin their communications with me with sentiments along the lines of, 'I'm speaking the truth here'; 'I'm not making all this up'; 'I have no reason to make all this up – it really happened'; 'Before this experience I didn't believe in life after death'; or, 'I really didn't imagine all this and I'm not going mad.'

It is obvious to me that all the people who write or talk to me about their afterlife experiences are not crazy. They are simply ordinary people with ordinary lives who have encountered something extraordinary. But there's been a lot of mind-blowing information in this chapter and I wouldn't be surprised at all if you still have niggling questions and doubts – it is human nature to do so. Indeed, I can almost hear you asking yourself, 'Is this really all for real?'

Again, I can't answer that decisively for you. All I can tell you is that to the people who have had visitations from the other side the experience was real. I also know that very few people who have had a vision of the afterlife actually worry about whether their experience was real or not, or whether alternative, more plausible explanations can be found. They don't question and doubt it in the way others tend to do, because all that matters to them is that the experience happened and it had a profound personal significance for them. It changed their minds and their lives for ever by showing them that a part of us survives physical death.

Of course, if you haven't had an afterlife encounter yourself you may find it hard to match this kind of personal conviction, but the fact that you don't think something extraordinary has ever happened to you does not mean that it won't ever happen. It could simply not have happened yet. Remember, visitation experiences can happen at any age or stage in life – there are no rules. The majority of people who contributed to this book didn't anticipate or expect what happened to them, but then out of the blue something happened and proved conclusively to them that there is an afterlife, and in that afterlife we are reunited with loved ones. The day before their experience these people would have woken up in the morning with absolutely no idea that their lives were about to change for ever.

The next chapter will introduce you to a truly fascinating and relatively modern category of afterlife communication stories: those that involve telephones and physical items.

CHAPTER FIVE

Calls from the Dead

If it happens, it is possible.

An unnamed law of the universe

Reported sightings of spirits date back centuries and are as old as humankind itself, but the same isn't true of many of the accounts in this chapter, because in each case the person involved is convinced they have received tangible communication from the other side through a telephone or everyday item. We aren't talking about sensations or feelings here, or even symbolism – as we will in the next chapter which focuses on subtler signs or messages from the other side – but about actual occurrences or observable events involving ordinary, everyday things that the observer did not imagine or even anticipate. I guess you could say we are talking about modern marvels or miracles. Something impossible happened.

I've given the chapter the title 'Calls from the Dead' because a lot of stories do involve phones, both fixed and mobile, but there are also stories about other inexplicable physical happenings. Even though what you are about to read is extremely powerful and convincing testimony in favour of the existence of an afterlife, I deliberately didn't place this chapter earlier in the book because, perhaps more than any group of stories in this book, the ones you will encounter here will stretch your imagination. Again, I'm not asking you to believe what you read. All I ask is that you open your mind to the possibility that there could be a supernatural explanation for unexplained events. I'm quietly confident that you will approach this chapter with an open mind because you've already read the previous chapters and have not abandoned the book. You're curious and want to read on, and a curious mind is an open mind.

Let's begin with stories about phone calls from the dead.

Making a connection

It may surprise you (it surprised me!) to discover that in the last century the subject of phone calls from the departed has been taken seriously by a number of psychologists and inventors and been fairly well researched and documented by respected scientists. The famous inventor Thomas Edison was fascinated by the idea of a person's spirit surviving death. This was due to his parents' association with spiritualism and also to the inspiration and encouragement he got from the work of British scientist Sir William Crooke, who claimed to have invented a camera to photograph spirits. Edison reasoned that, if it was possible to photograph spirits, then it must be possible to invent a telephone that could enable communication with spirits of the dead. In an interview for *Scientific American* in 1920, Edison said he was working on just such a project. He believed that the apparatus would be unpredictable and fragile but, despite this, it might offer the best possible chance of communication with the world of spirit. Sadly, Edison died in 1931 before he could invent his spirit telephone and there are no records or research records to prove he was actually working on it apart from his interview with *Scientific American*.

As far as academic research is concerned, the most significant documented research was undertaken by D. Scott Rogo and Raymond Bayless in 1979 for their book *Phone Calls from the Dead* and again in 2012 by Callum Cooper in his intriguing book *Telephone Calls from the Dead*. These researchers agree that the transcripts of the phone conversations often have similar traits. The phone may ring, usually when someone is doing a routine activity such as housework or just about to drift off to sleep. When they pick up the phone the voice they hear is instantly recognisable as that of a departed loved one. The voice may sound very clear but it can also sound distant as if there is a frail connection. There may be just a 'hello' or there may be a short conversation, warning or message, and when the conversation ends the person will not hear the deceased person hang up. There won't be any dial tone, just silence, as if the lines were dead.

John is utterly convinced his departed daughter Ann Marie spoke to him on the phone.

This Happened

I had been cutting the lawn for my parents, whilst they were both away visiting relations in Germany. So after doing that, I had a rest in my old house in the living room. It was so relaxing. Suddenly, I woke up with a bang of the *Evening News* coming through the letterbox. I took it through to the living room and put it down on to the floor. Then it just opened up at a page which tells you about churches and spiritualists. I always wanted to go to one, and try to see if I could get a message from my daughter, Ann Marie, who would now be thirty-four years old.

So I picked the receiver up and tried to get this number, but it just had a tone as if you can't get through, or wrong-number tone. I tried about four times to get through and then gave it a few seconds' rest and tried again. But this time when I picked up the receiver, a voice said, 'It's okay, Dad, everything is fine and I am watching you both.' This was my daughter Ann Marie speaking to me. She did say her name. Incidentally, my folks don't have a shared line. After this happened, I put the receiver back down again and when I tried to phone again right after that the line was clear. I managed to get an appointment at the spiritualist church, and was quite amazed with the message I got. So I hope you were touched with my story, as this actually happened.

John was not hallucinating on medication or even in a deep state of grief when this experience happened, and the same can be said for all the stories I was able to include in this book. In most cases, the phenomenon happened spontaneously and took them by surprise. This next story, from Saskia, is fairly typical of phone-calls-from-the-dead stories – again, if anything *can* be typical when it comes to after-death communication.

Daisy

I've never written to anyone after reading a book before but I just had to write to you and tell you about something that happened to me today. I would really value your opinion. Am I going mad or did heaven speak to me?

It happened around 2 p.m. last Thursday. I had just put my baby daughter down for a nap when my mobile rang. I picked it up and it was my friend Daisy. I hadn't heard from her for a good few months and was keen to hear all her news. She told me that she had been really busy at work and that she was sorry she had not got in touch. I told her it was fine as I understood that nappies and baby talk wasn't for everyone and I promised to hire a baby sitter soon so we could have a girls' lunch just as we used to before I had my daughter. She told me that she would look forward to that and I suggested getting a date in the diary. I put the phone down to get my diary but when I picked it up again the line was dead. There was no dial tone, just nothing. I tried calling her back but only got her voice message.

I tried calling Daisy again later that evening to organise lunch and this time her mother picked up the phone. I asked to speak to Daisy and she burst into tears. Daisy had died in a car accident two days ago!

I promise you, Theresa, that I did not imagine this call and I did not know at the time that poor Daisy had died. Do you think someone was playing a sick prank — unlikely as the voice I heard was definitely Daisy's — or do you think I got a call from the other side?

Saskia was very surprised when she got her phone call because she had no idea at the time that her friend was dead. She had not expected the call at all and she did wonder if she imagined it. Lucas also questioned his sanity when he got a phone call from his grandfather.

Yesterday

One morning when I was sixteen years old I was home alone because Mum was visiting Grandfather in hospital. The phone rang and I picked it up and it was my grandfather. He asked me to take care of my mum and to stay out of trouble. I told him I loved him and that I hoped he would get better soon as he was in hospital recovering from an operation.

Later that day Mum came back from the hospital distraught because Grandfather had died. I told her how glad I was that I had got to speak to him before he passed over — but Mum looked puzzled and told me that she had been with Granddad all that morning and he had been far too weak to make any calls. Then she asked me what time I got the call and I said about eleven thirty. My grandfather had died at eleven fifteen.

I'm sixty-seven years old now and I often think back to that morning. At the time I wondered if I was going nuts and I know Mum thought I was making it all up to make her feel better, but I swear to you that I spoke to my grandfather on the phone. I can remember the conversation as if it was yesterday.

Cara also had an astonishing experience. Here is her story.

Slipping Away

My daughter Ruby died seven years ago and barely a day goes by when I don't think of her. She died so young – just seventeen – and her death could so easily have been avoided. She was a good girl and we were very close. She would call me several times a day but she started to hang out with the wrong crowd and the phone calls became less and less frequent. I felt her slipping away from me even before she died. The police told me that her death was a terrible accident and nobody was to blame but I think other-wise. She had been out drinking with her 'mates' and somehow she fell over and smashed her head on a stone paving. She was rushed to hospital but there was nothing the doctors could do and she slipped away three days later. A part of me died with her.

I'm writing to you to tell you about something that happened a week after my Ruby died. I was in a terrible state, crying all the time and missing her so much. I longed to hear her voice again and tell her how much I loved her. The hospital and police had given me the bag she had with her when she died and I had placed it on my kitchen table. Several times a day I would sit by the bag and pull out the items in it – her purse, her mobile, her makeup bag – and just hold them close to me. They still felt warm and I was convinced I could smell Ruby's familiar perfume.

One morning I was sitting there holding Ruby's mobile in my hand and her purse in the other when I heard my mobile ring. I put Ruby's phone and purse down and went to get my phone. I could not believe my eyes when I saw that the number ringing me was Ruby's number. I think I went into shock for a few seconds and then I answered the phone. I heard Ruby's voice – it was so very faint – and she said, 'Hi, Mum,' as she always used to. At first I found it hard to speak but then I started to tell her how much I loved her and how much I missed her calling me like she used to with all her news. I could hear her trying to speak to me but the line was so very weak. And then there was silence. Not even a dial tone, just silence.

I went back to the kitchen table to look at Ruby's phone. I tried to switch it on but it was out of battery. Theresa, please write back to me as soon as you can to let me know what you think. I know grief does odd things to people and I would give my own life to have my Ruby back but this really did happen. I don't want to tell my husband about it as it would scare him and he would think I was losing it but I do want to tell you. Please write back.

I did write back to Cara immediately to tell her that she is not alone and that phone calls from the dead are a well-documented phenomenon now in paranormal research. I also reassured her that I truly believe Ruby was trying to get in touch with her on the phone to tell her that, even though she had slipped away to the other side, she would never truly leave her.

This next story is not perhaps the best example of a phone call from the dead but I'm including it here because it made the news headlines in the United States in 2008 and brought the subject of ghostly phone calls to the media's attention. Countless explanations were offered and feverish debate ensued. Was this a phone call from the dead? Read what was reported in the US media and papers such as the *Los Angeles Times* at the time and see what you think.

In California's San Fernando Valley on the 12 September 2008 at 4:22 p.m., a commuter train carrying over two hundred passengers collided at a speed of 83 mph with a Union Pacific freight train manned by three men. One hundred and thirty-five people were injured and twenty-five people died.

One of those who died in what became known as the Chatsworth crash was a man called Charles Peck – a forty-nine-year old Delta customer service agent at Salt Lake City International Airport. He hoped to move into the area so he could be closer to his bride to be Andrea Katz, and when the crash happened he was on his way to a job interview at Van Nuys Airport. Katz first heard about the crash on the radio as she was driving to the train station with Peck's parents and siblings – who lived in the Los Angeles area – to meet Peck.

It took twelve hours for emergency services to recover Peck's body from the wreckage but during eleven of those twelve hours Peck's mobile called his son, his brother, his stepmother, his sister and his fiancée. In all, his family members and fiancée received a total of thirty-five calls. When they answered all they heard was static and when they called back their calls went straight to voice mail. At the time the calls gave them reason to hope that Peck might still be alive and trapped somewhere in the wreckage.

The volume of calls promoted emergency and search crews to trace the whereabouts of the phone through its signal and to look once again at the wreckage and location where the calls were coming from. The final phone came at 3.38 a.m. about an hour before Peck's lifeless body was discovered. An autopsy report revealed that Peck had died almost instantaneously after the crash.

Of course, rational explanations such as phone malfunction can be put forward to explain this and it is also interesting to note that Peck's phone was never located after the crash – it was probably crushed or damaged. And, although unlikely, this could possibly have made it repeatedly call numbers stored in its memory. Unless the phone is discovered the mystery may never be solved, but one thing is clear: all the calls were from Peck's phone and, when his grieving family found out he was dead, knowledge of the calls brought them great comfort.

At the time, the publication of Peck's story encouraged dozens of people to get in touch with me with similar stories involving phones and in each case the person involved was absolutely convinced that they received a genuine communication from someone departed. Indeed, I've noticed a significant increase in stories coming in that involve phones, and this isn't really surprising, as phone communication is commonplace and often takes precedence over face-to-face interaction. Just hearing a familiar voice on the phone can give a degree of certainty and familiarity that might not be possible with other forms of afterlife communication, and it is possible that in some cases this is why loved ones in spirit are starting to choose phones – whether landline or mobile – as a preferred method of making contact. In other words, the world of spirit is keeping up with the times.

Calling out to me

Of course, when someone hears the voice on the other end of the phone there is typically no opportunity to record that voice, as it happens without warning. However, there are instances when the voice of a spirit can be captured and proof presented. I'm going to digress a little here and discuss electronic voice phenomena.

There have been a number of theories put forward to explain phone calls from the dead, and one of the most prominent is electronic voice phenomena or EVP. This is a process by which voices that the human ear cannot hear are picked up by phones, MP3 player, camcorders, answerphones or other electrical equipment. The voices are never heard on recording, only on playback. They appear to be identifiable as men, women or children and are said to be reasonably clear and to speak or sing in a number of different languages. If you are interested in hearing a sample or two, try these websites: http://www.evpsounds.com/evps and http://www.electronic-voice-phenomena.net/index.php.

EVP are captured voices of spirits on tape. Sceptics are quick to say that the voices are the result of static and white noise, but EVP researchers believe they are a form of communication with the dead. As we saw earlier, the inventor of the phonograph and the light bulb, Thomas Edison, believed that it might one day be possible to build a machine via which humans could communicate directly with the dead. Regrettably, Edison never completed his invention but in the years since his death repeated attempts have been made to record paranormal voices on tape.

There are thousands of EVP websites like those mentioned above, and if you check them out you will see that many people from all over the world truly believe that EVP offer direct evidence of life after death. But there are also many people who believe it can be explained rationally and that the sounds heard are susceptible to imaginative interpretation. Despite harsh criticism, EVP researchers continue to try to find ways to capture on tape something that will prove once and for all that there is life after death, and in the last few decades electronic voice phenomena have moved into other media, including TV, music players and computers. It's an exciting and constantly evolving field of paranormal research and something I am definitely keeping a very close eye on.

Both auditory hallucination and psychokinesis – when a person in a state of crisis or extreme grief consciously or unconsciously uses mind control to will a phone to ring or, in the case of EVP, projects their own thoughts onto a tape – have been put forward as explanations. It is argued that it is a natural human inclination to project meaning onto otherwise innocent or random sounds. In other words, the voices come from a person's sub-conscious. Theories like this must be taken seriously, but from the EVP stories I have read this doesn't seem likely, and to date neither sceptic nor believer has been proven 100 per cent right. There is no doubt that a lot of EVP incidents that have been put forward as hard evidence are controversial, but, if no satisfying natural explanation can be found, it would be equally unscientific to reject the paranormal as one of many possible explanations. In my opinion, although captured evidence has yet to yield defi-nite, scientific proof of the afterlife, I think at this early stage in research it does provide enough unexplained data to satisfy those who believe and to give sceptics something to think about.

I'm sure you will agree that this EVP story from Predag is intriguing.

The Speaker

My father died suddenly from a heart attack a year ago and since then I have often wished he would make contact with me in some way. I just wanted to know he was all right.

Today a strange thing happened to me. After work I wanted to listen to [the singer] Norah Jones on my stereo, and after half an hour I heard some mumbling. As some men were talking in front of our home, below the window of our living room, at first I wasn't paying attention, but over time the mumbling became louder. I pressed stop on the CD player and to my surprise I realised that this mumbling was coming from the right speaker. It sounded like a man speaking very indistinctly, and regardless of the volume position on the amplifier the mumbling was always at the same volume. Then I completely removed the CD player from mains power, but still the same mumbling was heard from the speaker. Only the CD player is connected to the amplifier so I don't know where the signal could come from. I turned off the amp and turned it on again after ten minutes, and I could hear mumbling again coming from the speaker. Again, I turned off the amplifier and returned after an hour. There was no mumbling any more. Five hours later, I turned on the amplifier again and I heard no mumbling.

Hi-fi and music has been my hobby for fifteen years and I've never experienced anything like this. I bought the amplifier five months ago, brand new. Maybe you'll think I'm crazy, but I think maybe that was my dad. I don't know. I really don't know. Anyway, he was a musician in his younger days. He played guitar, violin and trumpet, and over the summer he played with a band to earn some money for education. This hasn't happened again and I am sure that it was my dad. Thank you for listening.

In the overwhelming majority of cases I think that EVP stories like Predag's are so convincing that they can't be simply explained away as fraud, hallucination or malfunction. I also think that the more technology advances, the more likely I am to continue receiving such stories, which is very exciting.

Equally intriguing and on the rise is the phenomenon of text messages from the dead. Here is Lucy's intriguing account.

Sorry

Gradually in the past four or five years I have become, I suppose you could say, depressed but functional. My thoughts have been quite dark. I've never got on well with my mother. A lot of my problems stem from my childhood. She is elderly now and I have had to visit more often to help out. This has darkened my mood further and there have been times when I have been praying for an accident/illness to take me from this world in a respectable fashion. My sister, who killed herself when I was twelve, has also been in my thoughts. I have been cursing her for taking her own life because I know what it feels like to be left behind and couldn't burden my children and husband with that, even though I would like to run away sometimes.

Despite my depression in recent months I carried on with my life and my job as best I could for the sake of my family. I was visiting a couple during the course of my work when I had cause to use my mobile phone. The screen was a plain white light with the word 'sorry' in the top left corner. I puzzled out loud, thinking I'd had an incomplete text or had somehow knocked the buttons whilst the phone was in my pocket. Eventually, the person I was visiting said that I must have a spirit wanting to apologise for something. I pressed a button on the phone and the message disappeared. I have tried every button on the phone and can't recreate either the plain white screen or even the font that the word was written in. I know it was a message from my sister as that day was the anniversary of her death. I'm normally quite private about my past but I feel compelled to tell everyone, although no one knows how dark my thoughts had become before this happened and I won't ever tell.

In addition to stories involving actual phone conversations or texts from people who have died, I have also received stories from people about phones that aren't plugged in or are out of service or mobiles ringing that aren't charged. This story from Anthony is fascinating.

Celtic Soul

I am a forty-year-old man who was born in Birmingham, England, to an English mother (whom I know had a Celtic soul) and Irish father. Even as a child I always felt much more of an affinity with Ireland than England and have always considered myself Irish.

When I was eleven my parents and I moved 'back home' to Ireland and settled in Dublin. We lived in an area very close to a lot of my cousins whom I had grown up with, since as a child I always spent every summer on holidays in North County Dublin, by the seaside, with them all. My mother and father had lived through a rocky relationship for many years until my mother eventually decided to leave and move back to England about fifteen years ago.

Since that time I made sure I visited my mother in

England at least a few times per year and always spoke by phone to keep in touch. My mother had suffered ill health almost from the time she returned to live in England and that ill health gradually got worse as the years passed by. She died aged seventy-one on 13 March 2011 in hospital in Birmingham. Over the last year and a half of her life my ma spent only a few weeks at home and was in hospital for the rest of that time. I would visit every time she was admitted to hospital and over the last eight or nine months in particular, I was on permanent standby to get the next flight possible from Dublin to get to my mother's bedside, as many times we felt she only had days to live.

Many, many times over that period I would drop everything at home in Ireland and get to the hospital; after a few days her condition would improve and she would be stable enough for me to be able to go home, back to my wife and son, my job and the new house we were in the middle of building in the Roscommon countryside. I managed to hold myself together through working in Dublin (100 miles away from Roscommon), having to stay away from home and my family, two nights per week to cut down on travel time and permanently had a packed bag of clothes and my passport in my car ready for the next time I would get the call to get to Birmingham as quickly as possible.

On 12 March I took my wife to a music concert in Dublin to see the band the Script. My wife and son really like their music (I like them a bit) and have a friend who does security for them who managed to get me tickets. It was the first night out my wife and I had enjoyed alone in a long time and something we both really needed and really enjoyed. It meant we stayed in Dublin overnight at my in-laws house about ten minutes from Dublin Airport.

At around 7.30 the following morning I received another phone call from my brother in Birmingham saying Ma had deteriorated again overnight and I should get there as quickly as possible, although he did say it could be the same as the other times and he would call me back with any updates. I woke my wife and told her I had to get to Birmingham again as soon as I could, so we got up and started to look on line for the earliest flight to Birmingham. It was only then I realised that we had driven to Dublin in my wife's car, which meant my packed suitcase and passport were in my car 100 miles away in Roscommon. We would have to drive the two hours back there to collect the passport, which meant the first flight I could get would be from Knock Airport in Co. Mayo, forty-five minutes' drive from home in Roscommon.

The first flight would not leave Knock until 3.30 p.m. During our journey home I constantly checked my mobile phone for updates from the hospital and it was then a curious thing started to happen. As the day moved on my mobile phone (reliable as long as I had it) would be turned off every time I checked it for messages. I would turn it back on to find the battery was fine and there should be no reason for it to turn off. After collecting my bag and passport at home and giving a quick explanation to my eight-year-old son as to why Daddy had to go again so quickly, my father-in-law drove me to Knock Airport.

Again the mobile phone would turn off for no reason every time I tried checking it. I checked in at the airport and my father-in-law bought me a sandwich in the café as I hadn't eaten properly all day. It was then I checked my phone again to find it turned off. When I turned it on a message flashed that I had a voicemail. My heart ripped apart as I listened to the first word of the message from a cousin in Birmingham. I knew that the message was going to tell me that my mother had passed away within the last few minutes. She had died whilst I was checking into the airport to get to her bedside.

There is a shrine to Our Lady in Knock Airport which I sat in to cry and while I sat in silence on the plane journey over, all I could think about was why I could not have gotten there in time. I also knew that if I had not taken my wife to the concert in Dublin, or even taken my car with the passport in it, I would have got to my mother's bedside before she died. Over the weeks and months ahead I often told my mother in my mind, how sorry I was for not getting to her bedside in time but gradually I spoke to people in particular, about how my phone kept turning itself off during that day, as if I wasn't supposed to know.

I have slowly begun to believe that it was my mother's way of protecting me from the news as long as she could, also that I was meant to take my wife to the concert in Dublin as a reminder that my wife is so important in my life and that maybe my ma did not want to see any pain from me, which would have come from being at her bedside when she passed away.

One last thing is on the evening of 13 March when my

brothers and cousins and I left the hospital and then the church in Sutton Coldfield, Birmingham, after mass, we all went to the pub across the street from my mother's house. I stood at the bar with my two brothers (who always lived in England) to buy drinks for all the family who had supported us through the most difficult of times, when at my foot on the ground (inside a pub) lay a solitary pure white feather. I had heard the story of the white feather signifying an angel taking care of a loved one who has died and it gave me great comfort to know that Ma was okay and was still with us in spirit and would never be too far away.

Thank you for writing your book, I have always considered myself more spiritual than religious, even though I am Catholic. I find books like yours just make sense and really help us to understand why some things happen, which at the time don't make sense. I cried again writing this email but find it much easier to tell this story now. The mobile phone worked perfectly well for another week after my mother died and was never turned off when it should not have been. I did replace it for another model and have not had that experience again.

Here is Luke's touching account.

Unexpected

My wife died a week before our thirtieth wedding anniversary. She had a heart attack. It was all very sudden and unexpected and my only consolation was that the doctors told me she would not have suffered, or even known what was going on. I had hardly any memories of adult life without her. She was the most wonderful woman. I could write a book about her. One of her most endearing qualities was that you could never second-guess her. She had such a youthful spirit and was always urging me to seek adventure and magic in life. She was beautiful on the inside and the outside. Sure, we had our tough times, as any married couple has, but we worked through them and our relationship was the stronger for it.

Our being so close, you can imagine how black my life felt when I spent my first night without her, but I don't think I was alone and, after reading one of your books, I just had to send you my story. It must have been about two in the morning when I heard a ringing sound. Numb with grief, I just tried to blank it out but the ringing was persistent. It rang twenty or so times, then stopped for a few minutes, then started up again.

The ringing got louder and louder and it dawned on me that it was coming from my room. I got up and eventually tracked it down to under my bed. I'm not as agile as I used to be, so it took a while to crouch down and look underneath, and when I did I saw a smallish parcel wrapped in red ribbon. I picked it up and sat on my bed and saw that it was a gift to me from my wife. She must have bought it for my approaching fiftieth birthday. I tore it open and it was a mobile phone. I wasn't interested in that, I was only interested in the card my wife had handwritten. In it she told me that she loved me for ever and it was time for me to stop being so old-fashioned and to have my own mobile phone. My reluctance to use computers or own a mobile phone had been a source of constant discussion between me and my wife. She loved the technology. I hated it.

I grabbed the phone and held it to my heart and eventually drifted off into an uneasy sleep. The next morning I told my son he could have the phone because the card was all I really wanted. Hearing it ringing the whole night before was enough for me. My son took the phone and told me it couldn't have been ringing because it hadn't even been charged yet. While he was speaking I had a ringing sensation in my ears. When the ringing stopped I looked at my son and in that instant – don't tell me how – we both knew that this was my wife's way of reaching out to us from the other side, letting us know that, even though we couldn't see or touch her any more, she was still very much with us.

Hardly a day goes by when I don't draw comfort from that phone ringing. It rings quite a lot these days, as I took my wife's advice and learned how to use it. Each time I answer it or use it I feel indescribably close to my wife. I'm aware this may not make sense to a lot of people, but it makes perfect sense to me, because she always told me to expect the unexpected.

Naelene, who earlier in the book spoke about a visitation from her first husband Basil, also sent me this story about an afterlife communication from her second husband.

Connections

When I married again it was to a lovely man called Roy. We had twelve years together before he passed on. He was in hospital for a while before he died. He was very ill and my daughter took me home to stay overnight with her. One night I lay in bed worrying. Beside the bed there was an antique telephone that was used only as an ornament. During his working years Roy was employed by a telephone company, so he had a strong connection with phones. At quarter to five in the morning that unconnected phone rang twice. I could not believe it. I couldn't go back to sleep, so I got up and sat on a window seat until my family all got up and I could tell them what had happened. Twelve hours later at a quarter to five that afternoon Roy passed away.

Naelene believes that the ringing of the unconnected phone that night was a sign from the other side that her husband was soon to pass away, but, even though he was going to another place, the strong connection between them would never die.

I have never received a text or phone call from a dead person but I do know that the people who write to me are honest and sincere and have no reason to make these things up. I'm inclined, therefore, to believe that perhaps departed loved ones can sometimes manipulate electrical energy, sound waves and modern technology to produce this form of connection. I've also received stories from people who say they have received communications from the world of spirit on radios, on televisions and, as was the case for Louise in her story below, on computers.

I've Seen Her

After my twin sister died I was inconsolable. We did every-thing together and knew everything about each other – or so I thought. One day, about six months after the funeral, I went online and the image of my sister, Mary, appeared on screen. There she was. It was her. I saw her sitting in her bedroom typing furiously on her laptop. I was surprised as we were both outdoor types and I never thought she was that into computers.

Then the image suddenly vanished and a web address appeared on screen. I clicked on the link and discovered that my sister had been keeping a blog. I had no idea. In her blog she talked a lot about school, her friends, Mum and Dad and me. She talked about how much she loved me and wanted me to live my dreams. She also talked a lot about angels and how she always felt surrounded by them.

I understood then that all this was to help me know she was okay and still looking out for me. I didn't use to believe in angels but I do now. I know for sure that Mary isn't gone and that she is with me all the time. I know because I've seen her.

Once again we get that familiar certainty. Louise just knows that her sister reached out to her from the other side. The medium that Mary chose to communicate to her sister with may be modern but the reassurance and comfort a communication from the other side brought her sister are centuries old.

Theresa Cheung

Strange goings on

Let's move on now to discuss afterlife communications that involve physical or material objects other than communications devices. These stories are more common than telephone communications and typically involve clocks stopping, lights flickering, electrical devices turning on and off, pictures and photographs moving, objects appearing in unlikely locations, doors opening and so on. While I have no personal experience of telephone communication, I do have some experience of this phenomenon, and that's why I know that these happenings cannot always be explained away as coincidence, chance or imagination.

I could give you many examples, but one that stands out happened on the day of my daughter's first birthday. I was sitting in the kitchen looking at her birthday cake and instead of feeling happy at reaching this milestone all I could think about was my mother. How I longed for my mother to be there and how much I missed her! Once again, I felt myself drowning in a sea of guilt about the fact that I hadn't been by her side when she died. She had died alone. Whenever I begged for a sign of forgiveness from her and there was only silence I was convinced that she was angry with me for deserting her, for not being with her in her hour of need. In my heart of hearts I knew that my mother could never hate me, but I couldn't let my guilt go. The pain came gushing back to me in sporadic waves. Just when I thought I had come to terms with my regret, it would come back with a tidal wave of grief that knocked the joy out of me. And here again were the guilt and hurt, fifteen years after my mum's death, on my daughter's first birthday. Once again pain was hitting me hard and destroying my self-confidence.

I stared at my daughter's birthday cake and thought about my mother's final lonely moments before she died. I hadn't been there to hold her hand. I kept my hands busy by tidying the house but this didn't keep my mind busy and I remembered my mother crying the last few times I left her. Why hadn't I stayed with her? I tried to pull myself together but imagining my mother's tearful and disappointed face overwhelmed me.

My grief and hurt became so intense that I found it hard to breathe. I walked outside hoping that a gust of fresh air would help release the tension inside. It did help a little but when I stepped inside I got all the help I needed. There, placed in the centre of the kitchen table right next to the birthday cake, was a mug with 'World's Greatest Mum' written on it. I did not recall putting it there and know it wasn't there when I stepped outside, because I would have noticed it immediately.

To this day I don't know how it got there, as there was no one in the house at the time. I'd been given it about a year or so ago by my husband but had never used it because deep down I didn't feel I deserved the tribute. Instead, I packed it away in a dark and hidden corner of one of my kitchen cupboards. But here it was ready to use, and without any sign of dust on it. I put the kettle on to make a cup of tea and as I sat down to wait for it to boil I started to giggle. In my mind I could hear my mum saying, with a hint of laughter in her voice, that the mug was for her, not me! I knew in that instant that my mum had somehow made sure that mug was placed there to reassure me. She wanted me to know she would be there in spirit on her grand-daughter's first birthday.

This next story, sent to me by Peter a few years ago, is similar in some ways to the experience I had with the mug suddenly appearing out of nowhere, in that it suggests that our loved ones on the other side don't want to see us in pain or racked with feelings of guilt or despair.

Picture Perfect

My wife died because I had had too much to drink at a party and she drove home instead of me as she hadn't drunk much at all. It was winter and she slammed on the brakes too hard when she swerved to avoid hitting a cat in the road. The car skidded into oncoming traffic and even though my wife was wearing a seat belt she died from internal injuries. I was pretty bashed up too but I pulled through. If I had been driving I would not have tried to brake for the cat. I should have been driving that night but I wasn't.

The first year was the hardest to get through, as I couldn't let go of my feelings of guilt, even though my kids didn't think it was my fault at all. I couldn't forgive myself that easily for making the decision to drink that night knowing my wife was nervous of driving when the roads were icy. Two years on from her death I'm starting to forgive myself now and I want to tell you why.

It was the anniversary of my wife's death and I was welling up again. My daughter wanted me to spend the evening with her but I didn't want to, so I sat alone in my living room. I needed the silence but then I heard this crash coming from behind me. I turned around and my wife's picture had fallen down. It was a picture I had taken of her before we had the children and she looked so lovely in it [that] we had enlarged it and got it framed. I looked at the wall and the back of the picture and there was nothing wrong with the fittings, so I hung it up again and went back to sit down. It fell down again. I hung it up again. Ten minutes later it fell down again.

I was starting to get a bit spooked out, so I decided to do an experiment. I found a picture of the kids that had exactly the same fittings as the one of my wife and hung it up. I left it for an hour and it didn't fall down, so I got my wife's picture and put it back on the wall. A few minutes later it fell down. I put it back on the wall and called my daughter to tell her what was going on. My daughter came round to see for herself but the picture didn't fall. It stayed there.

Do you think this was my wife's way of letting me know that it wasn't my fault she died and that she is still close by? My daughter thinks it is my wife's way of telling me that I shouldn't have been alone on the anniversary and I should spend it with her.

This next story, from Sandra, also involves a picture.

On Edge

My dad died in 1981 – he had a massive heart attack when he was 61. The night he died, I was sitting with my mum and sister at home, just talking about Dad, when there was the noise of something falling in the hall. As you can imagine, our nerves were all on edge, so it really made us jump. I went into the hall and found a picture that Dad had bought face down on the floor. Now it had been hanging on a hook, and the only way it could have come off was by physically lifting it up and over that hook. It couldn't have just slid off, and the hook was still firmly in place. Also, despite the fall, the glass was unbroken. I think it was Dad trying to tell us that he was okay.

I can understand why some people might be doubtful about these kinds of stories. As soon as a picture of a departed loved one falls down, or a lost item is found, or lights flicker or a door opens by itself, the assumption is made that the other side is reaching out when it could just as easily be explained in a rational way. However, the quality and creativity of the stories I have received over the years, coupled with my own experiences, have convinced me otherwise. I am in no doubt that departed loved ones can to a limited extent manipulate electricity or objects to communicate to us.

Several people have written to me to tell me about music boxes or other mechanical items that were previously broken playing again and how they believe a departed loved one used that item to reassure them. Here is Russell's intriguing story.

The Force is With You

It was the morning of my GCSE maths and I was feeling horribly anxious. I'd worked hard but the previous year I'd missed quite a lot of school due to a serious chest infection. I had done my best to catch up but it had knocked my confidence quite badly. I wanted to try and go to university or college so I needed to at least get a pass in maths. It wasn't my strongest subject though and I knew it and my teachers knew it. Anyway, that morning as Mum cleared away the breakfast stuff I got a mini panic attack. I started to sweat and feel really sick. Mum felt my head and it was very hot. We were seriously considering ducking out of the exam when suddenly I heard 'The force is with you, young Skywalker' boom out from my *Star Wars* mug on the windowsill, which had a battery-operated voice pack. We both burst out laughing and I instantly felt better.

I'd got that mug about six years ago when I was deep into my *Star Wars* phase. Every time you lifted it up it would say, 'The force is with you' and play the *Star Wars* theme tune. I hadn't used it in years and it had just sat silently on my windowsill. My mum said it was the sunlight triggering the speaker but it had never happened before and I'm convinced my guardian angel triggered it to give me a welcome bout of humour and self-belief.

Russell emailed me a few months later to tell me that he got the results he needed.

Then there are stories about clocks stopping or restarting at the moment of passing or at specific times that have great personal significance for the person involved. Here is Frank's story.

Somewhere in Time

The pain of losing my wife to cancer when she was just fifty was so intense I didn't know if I could keep breathing, let alone continue with my life. My sister and my son were very concerned about me and discussed me coming to live with them on an alternate basis – one month with my son and one month with my sister – until I was able to cope by myself again. I wasn't able to think straight so just let them sort out the details. I never moved in with either of them, and let me explain why.

At my wife's funeral I was still in a deep state of shock. It didn't seem real that my wife wasn't going to be by my side any longer. Everybody was trying so hard to comfort me but I was beyond help. I just wanted my wife back. I hated the funeral service and when it got too much I went outside to get some fresh air. My daughter came running after me and told me I would regret it. I told her that I just needed some time alone and I would come to the reception afterwards at three o'clock. I went to our local park and sat on a bench.

I don't know how long I sat there but when I looked at my watch it was two-thirty. I didn't want to let my daughter down as I knew she was hurting just as much as me, so I reluctantly made my way back to the house for the reception. When I got there my daughter was furious as it was nearly five o'clock and all the guests had left. I looked at my watch and it was stuck at two-thirty, and then it struck me. My wife had died at exactly two-thirty.

Do you think that she stopped my watch to let me know that she was still around and to spare me the torture of putting on a brave face at the reception? She knew how much I hated these kinds of thing. My watch has never stopped before and the next day it was working just fine. It's amazing how a watch stopping has brought me such comfort and is helping me work through my grief.

The appearance of lost objects at meaningful times is another well-documented sign of afterlife communication. Kathy emailed me this story.

The Spoon and the Shoe

This experience occurred on Norfolk Island. Since the passing of my mum we now have a home there and use it for holidays. We have a child's cutlery set there that was mine when I was young and whenever my children were on holiday at my mother's place they would use this set. This particular visit I noticed that the spoon was missing. I asked friends if they had seen it as their family members had used the house prior to our visit. No, they hadn't. We had been there a couple of days and I was annoyed at the disappearance of this spoon. This particular day we had been out in the morning, all the dishes had been done and put away before we left and upon our return for some reason unbeknown to me I walked straight into the kitchen, I opened the drawer and there sitting carefully placed right on top was the spoon.

Another spirit visit occurred towards the end of that same holiday. Again we had been out and upon our return we found a pair of cheap foam slip-on shoes. I asked everyone that I knew if they had left a pair of shoes at our back door, but no one owned them. The strange thing is that they are well worn but when I put these shoes on they were perfectly moulded to my feet.

Another well-reported form of spirit communication involves lights flickering on or off or electrical devices suddenly switching on. Bill talks about his experience below.

Flickering

Two weeks after my uncle died I was in my living room reading when the lights started flickering. It was annoying me, as I couldn't read properly, so I got up to see if there was a problem with the switch. As soon as I got up the lights stopped flickering. I sat down again and the lights started flickering again. I got up and they stopped. This went on for about five minutes and it drove me crazy and then I remembered the chair game I had always played with my uncle when I was a child. In every room there was always a comfy seat – usually the one closest to the heating or the TV – and my uncle and I would identify it quickly and always try to make a dash for it first. It was our silly game and we shared so much laughter. Sometimes I won and sometimes he did and sometimes we ended up on the seat together, me sitting on his lap – until I got too old.

As soon as I remembered our chair game the light flickering stopped and it hasn't happened since. Do you think this was my uncle's way of saying goodbye?

In many cases the physical phenomenon is spontaneous but I also read a lot of stories from people – like Joan, whose account follows next – who receive this kind of communication when they ask for a sign or just long to know that their loved one in spirit is still with them.

Die Hard

Charles, my husband, died three years and two months and five days ago. I get very lonely without him. He was my soul-mate. The evenings are the hardest as we used to watch TV together and sometimes stay up very late. After Charles died I couldn't bear staying up late any more on my own, so I would go to bed before the news, but last night something happened which I had to write and tell you about. I'm still shaking with the excitement of it all.

I went to bed at about nine-thirty and found it hard to sleep. I would have done anything at that moment to have Charles with me one more time and I begged him to let me know he was close by. I saw and felt nothing and fell asleep crying, but then I woke up to the sound of voices. They were shouting. At first I got really scared, as I thought it might be an intruder, but then I realised that I must have forgotten to switch off the television, so I got out of bed and went to switch it off. I was always very careful about switching the TV off and unplugging it at night but I must have forgotten this time, so I went into the living room to switch it off. One of Charles's favourite movies *Die Hard [With a Vengeance]* was on. I sat down and started to watch it. As I watched I felt more at peace than I had done for several years. It brought back so many happy memories and I didn't feel so alone. At the end of the movie I switched off the TV and bent down to pull the plug out but the plug was already pulled out! How was that possible? I had just watched the end of a movie.

In my head I have gone over what happened that night over and over again. Was it me that pulled the plug out? Each time I come to the same conclusion. I did not pull the plug out after I watched the movie and I did not leave the TV on when I went to bed. I truly believe Charles had something to do with it and was sitting there with me that evening. He heard me crying and came back to reassure me. It has made all the difference. I know he isn't with me physically any more but now I feel him all around me all the time. It is wonderful, Theresa, just wonderful.

And sometimes, as was the case for Michelle in her story below, it is a combination or culmination of unusual physical events that brings an unmistakable conviction that those who have died are never far away.

Is He Still With Us?

My dad was diagnosed with incurable cancer in October 2006. My heart sank when I found out, as I was only twenty-three and the thought of losing my dad at a young age made me feel sick to the stomach, as I was always a daddy's girl.

At the time, my cat had kittens and my dad disliked cats. I however managed to convince him to keep the two kittens as comfort for my mum, in times to come. A couple of months later on the kittens were chasing each other and one jumped up and smashed my dad's favourite ornament of an Indian on a horse – my dad loved John Wayne and always watched cowboys-and-Indians films. The ornament was a present from me and my brother for his fiftieth birthday. At the time he was furious, as it was expensive and had sentimental value. He was so angry he threatened to send the cats away if it happened again (although I don't think he ever meant it).

A few months on, my dad's condition deteriorated and eventually, in October 2007, he became bedridden and was in a hospital bed downstairs in the front room. By this time he was unable to speak, just grumble, and could barely see. Suddenly, one night, he started grumbling really loudly and shaking his head as if he was trying to tell me something. He began to point up towards the top of the cupboard near his bed, and there was the broken Indian ornament. It was as if he was saying 'get that fixed' – although I didn't think too much into it at the time.

Two days later my dad died. I was devastated losing my dad at twenty-four years old and he was only fifty-six. I had never felt so alone, even though I had supportive friends and family. That night after my dad had died I stayed in my mum's room and, in the morning when we woke up, in the middle of my mum's bedroom floor was a picture of an Indian, face up, which belonged to my dad. I have no idea how it got there and we are both convinced it was a sign from my dad telling us to fix the ornament before his funeral, as there's no way it could have fallen down by itself because there was something heavy in front of it and had been there for years. Anyhow, Mum and I set about fixing it before his funeral.

After Dad's funeral I had been asleep at my mum's in my room when suddenly out of nowhere my alarm clock went off and everything on my shelf fell off, all at the same time. It startled me as this all happened at midnight exactly and I never used my alarm clock or set the alarm, especially not for midnight. I felt calm, though, as if I felt a presence and I think this and the picture falling was my dad telling me he was okay and he was still there.

Joan and Michelle share a wonderful certainty that a loved one in spirit is still with them. They truly believe that a departed loved one has reached out to them through a physical object or item and this has filled their hearts with joy and hope for life eternal. Their stories show that heaven can shine through even the most mundane and ordinary of things, like a picture or an alarm clock or a film on TV, and that at any moment our lives can change for ever as a result.

Making contact

Yes, all these stories are hard to explain and we must rely on the integrity of the people who sent them; but, as I have said many times over, all the people who write to me assure me they are telling the truth, and I have no reason to doubt them.

Also, as quantum science pushes our barriers of understanding of what is possible ever further, I am confident that one day we may be able to understand unexplained physical phenomena and even recognise them as legitimate forms of contact with the other side. Right now, though, it is still impossible to explain the phenomenon of phone calls from the dead, or how an alarm clock can go off on its own, or how a TV that is unplugged can switch itself on, or how an object can mysteriously appear at just the right moment when we need support. But one thing I do know is that for those who have been involved with the experience it is unforgettable. It offers them the courage and inspiration they need to cope with their grief and the hope that one day they will reunite with a departed loved one.

It also shows that communication with the other side is a very real possibility and that our departed loved ones can 'speak' to us in the most unexpected ways if we open our hearts and listen – and this possibility of communication from the world of spirit leads us neatly into the subject of the next chapter: subtle signs and messages from the other side.

CHAPTER SIX

Signs

There is no Winter harsh enough to withhold the promise of Spring.

Karen Kaiser Clarke

Phone calls from the dead, visions of departed loved ones
and near-death experiences are truly extraordinary afterlife
encounters, but in keeping with the spirit of honesty that
created this book I have to say that, although such direct and
unmistakable communications can and do happen, they are still
very rare and not everyone will experience them. Far more commonly experienced, however, are subtle signs that are intuitively
noticed and understood by some people as a communication
from the other side meant only for them.

But what are these signs, and are they really substantial
enough to be put forward as evidence for the existence of an
afterlife?

Signs are deeply personal messages that can reassure a

person that their departed loved one is still close by and very much alive in the world of spirit; and they can be anything you see, hear, smell or feel that feels like a message from the afterlife intended only for you. Many of the most commonly reported signs come from the natural world – feathers, rainbows, clouds, flowers, birds and animals – but they can also be material things such as small coins or lost objects found, as well as sounds, words and sensations that are heard, read or felt at exactly the right moment to bring solace.

Although signs are a fairly common type of after-death communication I deliberately didn't start this book with a chapter about them. This is because, as far as proof for the existence of heaven goes, I am fully aware that signs don't carry much weight; and, because of their personal nature, they certainly could not become the focus of scientific study in the way that near-death experiences, deathbed visions and phone calls from the dead are. They are a subtle, symbolic form of communication and the person involved must first notice and then understand and give personal meaning to them. However, despite not carrying as much weight as previous afterlife experiences mentioned in this book, signs can offer large numbers of people a great deal of comfort and reassurance that there is life after death. The stories of these people have a right to be heard.

The major problem with stories about signs is that, although for the person involved they feel like messages from heaven intended only for them at just the right time, for sceptics they can be easily discounted as random chance or mere coincidence. Chaos theory is often presented as the answer to anyone who believes that life is something more than a collection of random events, but it's worth pointing out that in the last few decades scientists have discovered a new meaning to chaos theory that suggests that there may indeed be subtle patterns to chaos. Take the miracle of DNA, for instance, or the human circulatory system, or the intricate design of a snowflake. There is nothing random here, just a perfect design in which everything has a place, function and purpose, and all the people who submitted stories for this chapter felt exactly the same way about the signs or coincidences that transformed their lives.

These signs were so well timed, so perfect and so deeply personal and meaningful to them that they had no doubt they were from the other side, bringing them clarity, hope and certainty out of chaos, pain and doubt, and offering them all the proof they needed that heaven exists. So, if scientists are even starting to argue that nothing in the universe is random, I truly believe that stories about signs do carry some weight and deserve their place in this book, because they add to the growing body of evidence that there is a higher purpose to our lives and that the afterlife is real.

The loss of a loved one is the hardest thing anyone will have to face emotionally in their life, but time and time again I have seen how this challenging and complex emotional journey becomes so much easier to bear when the person who is grieving receives a sign that death is not the end but a brilliant new beginning. Wendy, who spoke in Chapter Three about the death of her brother (see 'With Open Arms'), shows how tears can turn to laughter when a subtle sign appears.

Baby Feathers

After Steven's funeral I found a tiny white feather and immediately thought that Steven was getting his baby angel
feathers, and had come to let us know. I had a great laugh at
the thought of him dropping feathers everywhere as he got
used to them (and if you could see my 6 ft 3 in brother you'd
know feathers are not something he'd be comfortable with).

A few days later I was telling Mum about finding the
feather and the connection to heaven. We had walked down
the street to the shop as we talked and were on our way
back to the car, retracing our earlier steps. As I finished telling
Mum about angels, I saw a tiny white feather on the ground.
I stopped and pointed to it for Mum. Then we looked
around and saw hundreds of tiny white feathers everywhere
on the ground around us. We just stood there in amaze-
ment, as none of the feathers had been on the ground when
we'd walked that way about ten minutes earlier. They were
all very little, new baby feathers. We laughed about Steven
getting his baby feathers. It was great to laugh again after all
the pain and grief and to know that Steven was okay.

Although it isn't impossible – as the stories in previous chapters
have shown – it is still rare for spirits to materialise themselves
to us directly, probably because this takes up too much energy.
But there are many people, like Wendy, who know that they can
show themselves to us in subtle, deeply personal ways. The message might be a feather or a cloud or a bird hopping in your path.
It could be a rainbow or the lyric to a song heard at just the right

time to give you hope. It could be anything at all. And, if you are able to recognise and appreciate the sign as communication from the world of spirit, the brilliant thing is that you may start seeing signs and messages everywhere you go. It's a bit like a door: once you know how to open it you can see what is on the other side.

As they are so subtle and personal, it is small wonder that signs have not had as much attention as more physical and dramatic forms of spirit communication, but, from all that I have experienced of them – and read and heard about them in my mind – they are just as life-changing and overwhelming. I truly believe that we are surrounded by signs from the afterlife every day of our lives. The problem is that most people do not know how to notice and acknowledge them. Over the years, I have come across a number of gentle signs from my mother and father in spirit at important moments in my life, and in each case they were a source of profound inspiration and guidance. They not only helped point me in the right direction, but were also a source of great comfort. However, since I was a late developer spiritually, it took a while for me to notice these signs and to understand and be guided by them. I'm hoping that reading this chapter will help you notice, understand and interpret the gentle, reassuring signs that are being revealed to you all the time. The details and circumstances may differ but in each case the message delivered is the same: our loved ones are still alive in spirit.

Perhaps one of the best-known signs from heaven is the discovery of a white feather. Whenever I come across a white feather I'm mesmerised. I take a moment to pick it up and ponder the eternal life that awaits me after death. I feel a huge inner smile rising and a warm, all-embracing certainty that nobody who has experienced it can easily deny. Many people may find it hard to believe that a small feather can have such a profound impact, but, as Clare's story shows, feathers can not only be a sign that those we have lost and loved are all around, they can also touch your heart.

Feathers brush my heart

People have said to me that there is nothing harder than losing a child – and they are right. I should know, because I lost my son when he was only fourteen years old.

I was told that he had died by a doctor in A&E The accident, which involved twelve people, had left three young boys dead and one adult, the driver of the coach taking them to their athletics trials. I had to identify my son for the officials. I was in a state of shock and I was in the morgue. I was in a sterile, brightly lit room and my son and his best friend were lying on white sheets. As I gazed down at his body, as beautiful in death as he was in life, I didn't have any desire to touch him because I knew he was no longer here. I just silently and carefully said farewell to the body I had loved and taken such great care of.

Ever since both my children were born I made sure that they had only the very best – the best food, the best education and the best home I could provide. I raised them on organic produce and taught them to love and respect the earth and their bodies. My son became a gifted athlete. He excelled at school sports and was soon competing nationally. The shelves of his untidy room were crowded with cups and awards. When he was young, as children often like to do, he would bring me little gifts from the garden: a snail, a daisy, a rose and one day a feather. I treasured every one of his gifts and whenever he brought me a feather I told him that it belonged to an angel. His face lit up and from that day on he was forever bringing me feathers that he found on his way to and from school. He even found one on the path the morning he left for his final trip. I still had it in my pocket as I stood over him in the morgue.

In the days before the funeral I carried the feather with me everywhere I went. Holding it somehow comforted me. As they lowered the coffin into the ground, with tears running down my cheeks I gently let the feather go and watched it flutter onto the coffin lid. Then a gust of wind blew and the feather returned to me. I kissed it and let it go again and the same thing happened but this time it flew back onto my coat and rested just above my heart. I knew then that my son was sending me a sign.

I had survived the worst thing that can happen in a mother's life, but I had also experienced the greatest gift, the never-ending love of my son. He is and always will be the feather that brushes my heart.

This poignant and moving email was sent to me by Lucy.

Three Feathers

I would like to share my recent experience with you also, Theresa. Last December, 2010, I lost my brother. He was in his early thirties and the youngest of our family. It was a huge blow to all of my family. I have four sisters and one other older brother. My younger brother suffered with severe anxiety for the last few years and more recently depression. It all became too much for him last December. As you can imagine, it was a very painful experience for all of our family to go through, especially my mum, as she was very close to my youngest brother. He was single and had lived at home all his life.

The months following my brother's death had been very difficult for my mum in particular to endure. She was a woman of great faith (we are all Catholic) and she felt that God had really let her down. Mum had prayed all her life for her children – their wellbeing, health, exams etc. – and now the rock that she had placed so much trust in had 'failed' her. She was utterly devastated. My dad and my siblings all felt my brother's absence too of course, but we were able to cope better than my mum. It was very hard to see her in such mental pain. I think she also greatly feared that my brother may not have gone straight to heaven and that worried her enormously also.

I prayed hard every day that she would get the strength she needed to face each day a little stronger. I also prayed to her guardian angel that she would look after her and wrap her angel wings around her with the love and support she needed to carry on. The other day, after reading your book, I asked the angels to send me a sign that my brother was okay and that he was safe and happy and hopefully in heaven. A couple of days later, I was walking along a beach and I came across three beautiful white feathers close together. I knew this was the sign I was looking for. The three feathers symbolised that my brother's soul was and is still very close to my parents and that he is now happy and free of the mental torment that he endured on Earth due to his illness.

The appearance of a white feather also brought Maureen great comfort.

My Lifeline

My husband Eric and I were married for forty-four years when he was diagnosed with prostate cancer. I can't tell you what a shock it was and very upsetting. Well, my story begins with Eric and I watching a TV programme about how white feathers can sometimes appear when someone dies.

Not long after, in November 2003, Eric sadly passed away. The following April my family said that we should go away to Tenerife, as it was a place that Eric and I loved going to every April. I'm sure it was what he would have wanted me to do. Of course, we knew it was going to be very hard and upsetting without him and it was. But a strange thing happened. I was out on the patio of our apartment when a small but pure white feather landed on my hand. There wasn't a single bird in sight. I truly believe that this was a sign of Eric's approval of my holiday. I still have the feather and will never part with it as it is my life line.

Feather signs will often appear when you least expect them, and typically there will be no logical reason for their appearance. They will just be there as if someone placed them there for you to notice. Whenever I talk about feathers as one of the most common signs from the other side, there are always those who say that it is just a feather and not a divine message. I'm quite sympathetic to this point of view but then I read stories like those from Maureen above and I have no doubt that they are a communication from the other side. A white feather also brought Cheryl solace. Here's her story.

Made Me Smile

My grandma lost my granddad ten years ago this February just gone. It was a very difficult month for her as it is also her birthday and the month she was due to finish her chemotherapy for bowel cancer. As a surprise we got all the family together for a meal, even the ones who live out of town and her two baby great grandchildren, to celebrate her birthday and the end of her chemo.

During the day we all talked about my granddad and the holidays we went on and how proud he would be of my grandma fighting the cancer. When I got home, there on the middle of the sofa was a small pure white fluffy feather. I know we didn't bring it in with us as I went straight into the living room alone, and it couldn't have been blown in through a window as it was a cold February day and we hadn't had any windows open. I told my grandma about the feather and we both believe it was a sign from Granddad letting us know he was with us at the meal and he was proud of my grandma.

Siobhan would also like to share her story.

So Beautiful

Upon reading your book I decided to let you know my story. I had been dating a guy I knew from my childhood for the last fourteen months. His name was John and we both had come out of sad and traumatic relationships before we got together. John had taken me out of a rut and I did the same for him, and then I saved up and got him his first passport and took him to Medujorie. It was there that John had a vision of his beloved mam, who had passed over during our time together. John had been very close to his beloved mam and never really got over her passing. My John had lived more in the fourteen months we were together than in his thirty-nine years.

Three weeks ago I called to pick up John and as I entered his kitchen I saw that John had placed three framed pictures – two of us and one of his mam. There was also a letter for me. It was then I found my John dead. He had hanged himself. I was so distraught but the reason I am writing to you is the next morning on the windscreen of my car there was frost but nowhere else. As I got into the car I noticed it was full of angel feathers. I have never seen anything in my life so beautiful and knew at this stage it was my John letting me know he was okay. I took a picture of the feathers and if you wish to see it will send it on to you. I do miss him so much and cannot believe he's gone but know in my heart he is around me all the time protecting me like he said he would in the letter he left behind for me.

So eleven months after his mam going John went to be with her. God bless and thank you for taking the time to read my story.

Signs in the sky

Two other well-reported signs or messages are rainbows and clouds. Rainbows always seem magical. They make us pause and stare. They draw us in, and these feelings of awe and inspiration can open up lines of communication with the world of spirit, as this next story from Petra shows.

Magical

On the morning of Dad's funeral I didn't think I could face the day. I dragged myself out of bed and pulled back the curtains. It was a really dreary day and it mirrored my mood. My husband brought me a cup of tea and I just sat there by the window staring blankly. I couldn't imagine life without Dad. I couldn't believe that he had gone.

Eventually I got dressed and went downstairs for breakfast. I barely touched my food and then the doorbell started ringing as relatives and friends arrived. I should have been grateful for their care and devotion to me but at that moment I really didn't want to be around anybody, not even my husband, so I sneaked outside into the garden and hid behind the shed. I was wearing slippers and got them very wet, as it had been raining, and I didn't have time to change my shoes. I started to have a smoke and then as I was standing there behind the shed I felt a shaft of sunlight on my face. It wasn't very strong but it felt so warm. I looked up and there in the sky was the most stunning rainbow I have ever seen. It had so many rich and vibrant colours. I stood there admiring it for a good ten minutes before I heard my husband calling for me. I knew it was time to go back into the house, so I stubbed out my cigarette and took one last look at the rainbow. It was truly magical.

I started to walk back to the house and as I did I felt pounds lighter. The feelings of darkness and dread had gone too. I can't explain it but I felt joyful. I knew with absolute certainty in that moment that Dad had gone to a better place. It was incredible and I will never forget it. In your books you talk about rainbows being angel calling cards and I often wonder if this was Dad's way of saying goodbye and helping me to cope with my grief. I told some of my friends about what had happened and they said it was just a rainbow, but it was so much more than that to me.

Of all nature's symbols, rainbows are among the most awe-inspiring, and one thing I have noticed from reading so many afterlife stories over the years is that, whenever there are feelings of awe, heaven is never far behind. Clouds can also bring feelings of wonder with their constantly changing shapes, colour and beauty. As a child, who has not lain down in the grass and done some cloud watching, searching for images? For some people, like Jill below, the images are so clear, so dramatic, that it can only be interpreted as a sign from heaven.

Big Heart

My little brother died when I was seven years old. He was only three and my parents did not want me to go to the funeral as they thought it would be too much for me. Instead, I stayed with a neighbour who had a daughter the same age as me. On the afternoon of my brother's funeral I don't remember much but I do remember it being a really sunny and beautiful day and lying down in the grass watching my friend play on her trampoline. She wanted me to come and play with her but I didn't want to. I remember looking up into the clouds and seeing this heart shape. My little brother always used to wear a T-shirt with a big heart on it and it really felt like he had put that shape in the sky just for me.

Butterflies and flowers

Along with rainbows and clouds, the appearance of butterflies at significant times is another afterlife sign I get a fair amount of mail about. It's not surprising, really, when you consider that butterflies are a symbol of spiritual growth and transformation due to the fact that they begin their lives as caterpillars that crawl on earth but then they transform into beautiful creatures that can fly. For Humberto, they are a symbol of hope.

Beautiful Day

On the day of my beloved mother's funeral it was hot and beautiful and then it started raining, like tears from heaven. Afterwards, we left to meet at my brother's house and outside my girlfriend and I encountered a beautiful butterfly. It was brown and had a beautiful red belly, more like a mariposa. The butterfly was so tame and even sat in the hands of my girlfriend first and then mine. It wasn't at all afraid and didn't seem to want to leave us. Could the butterfly be a sign from my mum?

I have also had a number of stories sent to me by funeral directors and undertakers who have noticed butterflies behaving unusually or unusual numbers of butterflies clustering around coffins prior to or during a funeral.

Flowers that bloom far longer than they normally would, or bloom at times they don't normally bloom, or come back to life after they have withered and died are another significant sign. Ashley wrote me this email a week after his mother died.

Red Roses

Theresa, I thought you might be interested to hear my short story. It is about a bunch of red roses that were sent to me after Mum died. My mum's name was Rose, so as you can probably imagine I was sent a lot of roses for her funeral, but something about this particular bunch of red roses warmed my heart and reminded me a lot of Mum, so I decided to keep them and give the rest away to a local hospital.

One morning, a few days after the funeral I noticed that the roses were starting to fade away and this made me feel very sad, as it seemed to underline the fact that my mum had gone for ever. The next morning the roses were in full and beautiful bloom again and they stayed like that for weeks. It was incredible and it really made me feel that Mum was sending me a sign to let me know that she hadn't died.

Objects and numbers, music and words

Birds appearing at unexpected times or behaving unusually are another relatively common sign, but it is not just the world of nature that can send those who are grieving the loss of a loved one a sign. Inanimate objects can also bring comfort, as this next story from Jackie describes. In many stories about signs, the people involved don't typically ask for a message. It just happens or appears spontaneously. But in this story you will notice that Jackie requested a sign.

Housework

Reading your book inspired me to share a story with you. It was something that happened to me a few years ago. I used to do housework for an elderly gentleman whom I will call Lenny; I also used to do the same for a couple a few doors up the street in a house with the same layout as Lenny's.

Lenny had always had a fear of dying and death and refused to go to the funerals of his friends who had passed over. One day when I was vacuuming in the hallway at Lenny's I noticed a pound coin up against the skirting board. I picked it up, handed it to Lenny and thought no more about it.

A few months later Lenny became ill and died in hospital. A week or so after his funeral I was vacuuming the stairs of the couple up the street from Lenny's house when I remembered how scared Lenny had been of dying and death. I said to myself, 'If you are okay, Lenny, please give me a sign,' and then I carried on with my work. When I reached the bottom step something caught my eye and there up against the skirting board, in exactly the same place as the one that I had found in Lenny's house, was a pound coin. I felt a tingle from the top of my head right down through my body as I remembered the pound coin I found in Lenny's house. I felt sure that this was my sign.

Coins suddenly turning up at just the right moment are yet another well-reported afterlife sign, but I've also had stories about a shaft of bright light suddenly appearing or shining on a coffin, an object or even a person during a funeral or memorial service, as well as lost objects found and flickering lights. The world of spirit may also use creative or even humorous ways to get our attention. One story I was sent told the story of a funeral and how tears turned to laughter when a Crazy Frog ringtone went off. The person who sent me the story felt this was a sign because the person they were burying had a great sense of humour and would not have wanted such solemnity at their funeral.

Departed loved ones may also choose to speak to us through the media. Time and time again I'll turn on the TV or the radio and hear someone say something that reminds me of my mum when I am really missing her. Or I'll be mulling over a problem and wishing I could talk to Mum about it and find myself inexplicably drawn towards buying a newspaper or magazine I don't normally buy, only to find that there is a message or piece of guidance waiting for me there. Another unexpected place to find reassurance is through numbers. The reappearance of the number 11 or multiples of it as 22, 44 or 55 is a well-reported sign.

Or perhaps comfort comes through the medium of music. Many people have written to me to tell me that, at times when they have been deep in grief, they have turned on the radio or walked into a shop and heard a song playing that they have associated with a departed loved one, and this has healed their heart. Books can also appear at just the right time to bring comfort and belief in an afterlife. It humbles me whenever I receive emails like this one sent to me by Faye.

Hazel

I am usually a person who likes to be out and about but today I had absolutely no inclination to do anything. I just wanted to stay at home and be peaceful. I have had a lot of stress in my life lately and I just wanted sit outside, enjoy nature and be quiet. I had a copy of your book and I took it into the garden to read.

I couldn't believe it when I came to the part about highly sensitive people. Most of my adult life I have suffered with bad nerves. As I reached my mid-forties I became even more sensitive – developing multiple chemical sensitivity and electromagnetic sensitivity. Aromas of all kinds gave me migraines, bright lights and loud noises affected me and I hated being in crowded places. Being outside in nature, walking on the beach or alongside the river became my favourite pastimes. I felt so relieved when I read that many people are like me. I am drawn to spiritual books like yours and this particular one had not just one message for me but two. I was reading the story 'Ending in a Hug' about someone feeling their departed mum around them and wishing that I had some contact from my mum, who died two years ago. I often spoke to her in my mind but didn't seem to get a reply. I couldn't believe it when I looked at the page – the next word after that story was Hazel. My mum's name was Hazel. I felt so happy after reading that.

And Andy sent me this email.

Andrea

I thought I would contact you with my story. My younger sister died last October. She was thirty-nine and had breast cancer. We were very close.

The Afterlife is Real

Well, to cut a long story short, I have always believed in angels, having seen one when I was two or three. Last night I picked up your book (which my youngest daughter had bought me on Saturday, she was also very close to my sister). I had been talking to my sister, as I do, asking her to contact me, when I opened the book on a random page and I then knew she was around, because the story on that page was about a lad who had a guardian angel tattoo, but the most amazing thing is that it said the road and place he was from was Stalls Farm Road, Droitwich. My sister was born in a house in Stalls Farm Road, Droitwich, and, if that was not enough of a message, I then turned to another page and there was a message that had been sent to a lady from her granddad. It read, 'Don't worry, Andrea, I'm fine. I love you so much I will always be watching over you. Take care and remember I will always be at your side wherever you are. I love you.' My proper name is Andrea. If only I could tell you how I felt. I always believed she was with me, now I know.

Take care and thank you.

Andy (I never liked the name Andrea, till now!)

This book may be your afterlife sign. It is in your hands for a reason. Many people have told me about the unexpected way one of my books came into their hands. They found it on the Tube or the cover caught their eye even when they were not looking to buy a book. Or a friend gave it to them as an unexpected present. Believe me, you were meant to read this book.

In this next story an unusual sign gave Tracey a sense of comfort and joy no amount of grief counselling could give her following the death of her granddad.

Bevan

In May 2008 sadly I lost my granddad after a week-long battle fighting an inoperable twisted bowel. To explain the importance of my story I think I should first set the scene about the relationship I had with my granddad. He had been a massive part of my life since childhood and in some ways was more like a father figure than a grandparent; he was someone I could go to for advice, always being a wealth of knowledge and full of interesting stories. I could sit for hours with him drinking tea and making small talk, together with my grandma. We always ended up laughing. Those are fond and happy memories. On a serious side, though, after being abandoned as a three-day-old baby and brought up by strict adoptive parents until he joined the RAF as a young teenager, my granddad could be a stern and serious man with strong morals, very quick to put you in line and speak his mind. The wonderful thing about Granddad, though, was even after a strong word from him, minutes later he would be cracking a joke, acting the fool and making us all laugh; that's what I loved so much about him, the laughter!

We sat by his side in hospital, day in, day out, and I held his hand tight as he took his final breaths on this earth, the day my earth fell apart. I've never felt grief the way I felt that day and, as dearly as I loved my other grandparents, never felt such savage emotional loss since. The hours and days following his death were a blur of utter loss and despair. I was consumed with grief and couldn't possibly imagine life without my granddad, and I went through the whole textbook denial, anger and depression symptoms of bereavement and was struggling to find the acceptance.

On the evening of his death I went home and curled up in my bed and lost myself in my own thoughts, memories and fears, somewhere I could not conceive a way out of. Later that night there was a knock at the bedroom door and in walked my best friend of many years, Lindsey, who unannounced had travelled 250 from South Wales to be by my side. She stayed with me for a week and, never leaving my side proved to be my rock. She had also been a great friend of my granddad.

After Lindsey went home I plummeted back into the darkness of my grief and started to feel an ever-increasing guilt for my grandma, mum and brother, who also had had a huge hole left in their lives. I felt I was not being strong for them. I had to see my GP to sign me off work as I knew I was not ready to return. My GP was very sympathetic and his parting words of advice to me were, 'The worst thing you can do is sit at home. Get out and be with friends and family.'

As I left my place of work that day after I dropped in my medical certificate signing me unfit for work for two weeks, the one question on my mind was, 'What should I do with my two weeks to best follow the GP's advice?' My first instinct was to go to South Wales to be with my friend. I knew she would be able to help ease my grief. But I felt so uneasy about leaving my family. How could I abandon them at such a sad time? My mind was tormented by thoughts and I didn't know what to do.

I was sat in my car waiting at the traffic lights outside my office when my eyes focused on the lorry in front of me. Right in front of me in my line of sight on the tailgate of the lorry were two stickers, one with the Welsh dragon and directly below it another with the word BEVAN, my grand-dad's surname! I instantly felt a surge of energy run through me and I knew this was a message from my granddad telling me I must follow my instinct and go to Wales.

Needless to say, I did as I was told and spent a week with my friend Lindsey in Wales. I returned feeling much more optimistic about the future and ever so slightly stronger and empowered to go forward and deal with my grief in a positive way and be with my family to help them with theirs.

The following year in memory of my granddad I completed a sponsored hike up Mount Snowdon in North Wales, raising just short of £300 for Barnardo's children's charity, a charity which had been close to my granddad's heart following his difficult childhood. I released a balloon that day on the summit of Snowdon with a card attached with a note to my granddad. Every year on the anniversary of his death I release a balloon up to sky and feel love in my heart for the gift I had for twenty-nine years of my life – my granddad!

I have always been fascinated by stories of signs from the other side and feel this proves my granddad was communicating to me that day at my time of despair, something three years on I look back on and recognise as a massive turning point in my life.

For Kathy, whom we heard from in Chapter Five (see 'The Spoon and the Shoe'), the sign and the comfort she needed came through the words in a poem.

Extremely Close

My mother and I were extremely close. I am married with two beautiful children and a great husband who my mother also loved. She became terminally ill and so my family and I went to Norfolk Island to care for her until she passed away. It was a very difficult time due to seeing her suffer and other difficult family issues.

After her passing, I went through all the emotions and was extremely hurt. We were at church and instead of listening I was thinking about Mum with tears streaming down my face. We were at the back of the church and with no thought I turned and picked up a book off the shelf. I had never done this in the past and have not done this since. I opened the book without thinking about what I was doing, and opened directly to a poem called 'Miss Me But Let Me Go', author unknown. The picture behind the poem was in pink and the scene could have been a typical one on Norfolk Island where my mum grew up and spent all her life.

And when I read the poem it sounded just like it was my mum talking to me. Of course I then had a river running down my face. But as days went by I became more at peace with things and emotionally I became more settled.

And in many cases it is not just one sign but a number or series of deeply personal signs that brings reassurance and comfort. Here is Gloria's heartfelt story, in her own words.

Beautiful Messages

I don't speak English very well. I'm helping with a translator. Forgive the mistakes! My name is Gloria and I'm fifty years old. I'm Italian. Just over a year ago my mother that I loved so much died and since then I have had great interest in that which concerns the spirit, love for God.

Mom sent me so many signs to let me know that she has not left me ... white feathers falling from the sky ... suddenly all butterflies that alight almost on me, but the extraordinary thing was a few days after her death the bedroom door of the hotel where we were staying gently filtered open and shone a bright light golden. I rose up suddenly turning on the light scared, thinking someone had entered the room but they had not. My husband reassured me and I feel asleep again, but this morning he told me that in the night he had seen the same light come through the door but when he got up to close the door it was closed already.

I think it was a beautiful message from my mom. I leave

my heart open to what that will be, I stay listening ... I feel an immense joy, sometime I cry for the emotions and the love I feel.

Helen sent me this story about the signs that reassured her.

Don't Stop Believing

My dearest nana passed away nearly five years ago and I miss her dearly. On 20 February 2012 it would have been her birthday, so I decided to go outside and have a chat to her. I told my nan that I loved her, missed her and, hoped she was having a good birthday. I begged her to show me a sign that she was okay. Well, after a few minutes I looked up at the sky and there was a cloud and at the end of the cloud was a shape of a heart, but not fully formed at one side. I was amazed and gutted I never took a photo. Then the cloud just disappeared but when I went back into the house I heard my favourite song, 'Don't Stop Believing', playing on the radio. I still think about this every day.

Norbury believes heaven is all around her.

Nearby

I was recently single and finding it tough, especially emotionally. It had been my decision to end it but suddenly being a single parent was daunting. I would constantly have toys work that no longer could work, knocks at the door when no one was there, doors closing right before our eyes with no rational explanation. I always wondered if it was one of my four grandparents who were passed. One day at work (I work at a kindergarten) I was telling a friend about my weird goings on when all of a sudden the radio, which was switched off, came on all by itself. My friend was shocked and didn't know what to do … Shortly after, one of the children came up and asked us what the man was doing there. When we asked her what man, she told us the man was standing near us and he was smiling. On further questions she described what he was wearing, exactly how my grandfather always dressed! My friend was spooked, but I was also comforted by him being there.

I'm indebted to Carla for sharing her experiences below.

Believe

I am emailing from far afield as South Africa and feel that I have to convey my experiences. A few days ago I decided to go to our local bookstore. My son was busy reading a magazine when my eye was drawn to your book *An Angel Spoke to Me*. That day I was feeling a bit down in the dumps as my birthday was coming up soon and although it should be a happy time I always found it sad as my sister-in-law died a day after my birthday. When I started reading your book, it felt as if she had guided me towards it. I immediately purchased it and cannot stop reading as I relate to most of the stories.

The Afterlife is Real

I definitely believe that spirits do exist because of the many incidents that have occurred over the past few years. In my experiences spirits have communicated to me via radio, number plates and dreams. I feel quite fortunate and love knowing that all my departed loved ones are constantly watching over me.

The first incident was when my husband was transferred to the same city where his youngest sister, Fern, lived. The first few times we put off relocating but this time my intuition told me that it was the right time to move. A few months later Fern was diagnosed with stage four cancer. One particular evening on our way to a healing service a car pulled in front of us with the number plate BELIEVE. Before I could show it to my sister-in-laws the car disappeared.

Throughout the coming months I had this strong feeling that she would be healed. However, on 2 September, a day after my fortieth birthday, Fern died. When this happened I became quite angry at God for not healing her in the way that we thought He would.

A few weeks later we were transferred back to our hometown. I believe my husband's mom had a hand in this, so that we could spend this short time with her. A day after her funeral our family gathered together for Sunday lunch and my other sister-in-law mentioned that on her deathbed Fern said that she would come back to visit us as a butter-fly. Well, that Sunday the mood around the table was very sombre. I was feeling very emotional and decided to take a walk in the garden. Lo and behold a butterfly came to sit on my arm. Another incident occurred while passing a Gospel bookstore. I felt this urge to enter the shop and walked towards a table with books that were on sale. To my surprise there on the table lay a pink notebook with butterflies and the word BELIEVE on the cover. On other occasions I would be sitting in church and thinking of Fern and the organist would play the hymn that we sang when Fern and I attended a course at her church.

Coming to my late father-in-law and father – they were both smokers and often I would get the smell of smoke while lying in bed at night. One time I decided to ask my husband whether he also smelt it but he could not. Yesterday on my birthday I was looking through old photo albums and decided to have two photos developed of Fern on her wedding day as her seventh anniversary is today. A few minutes after I dropped off the photos her wedding song 'You Raise Me Up' played over the airwaves. This made my day as I knew she was with me.

Finally, I constantly dream about Fern and she reassures me that she is happy and healthy where she is. I think she knew how hard I took her death and that I had feelings of hurt and anger inside me. A few months ago she visited me again but this time to tell me that it would be her last visit. Since then I haven't dreamt about her. Each and every time when I would dream about her I would convey this to my sister-in-laws, who would ask me why Fern only came to me in dreams and not to them. It is such a relief knowing that others also experience these visitations from their angels and that I'm not the only one.

Carla mentions dreams in her final paragraph and dreams of departed loved ones are yet another well-reported form of communication from the other side. I would love to discuss dreams of the departed in more detail here, and how they too are a perfectly valid form of afterlife communication, but that will have to wait until my next book.

This next story, from Karen, also reveals the true magic and power of coincidences, or, as I prefer to call them, signs from heaven.

An Angel Sang to Me

Having read your inspirational book *An Angel Spoke to Me*, I wanted to share my story with you. This is the story of my friend passing away and a series of 'coincidences' connected to this. My story starts in late 2009 when for my husband's fiftieth birthday I bought him a champagne balloon ride in the Cotswolds. A few months after his birthday we booked a weekend away in Gloucestershire with the intention of going up in the balloon. However, ten minutes prior to our flight time we were informed that due to poor weather conditions we would not be able to take the ride as planned. We therefore enjoyed the rest of our short stay and planned to reschedule the ride to a later date giving us reason to book another enjoyable short break in an area we love.

In June 2010 Margaret, a very dear friend of mine, passed away after a long illness. A few months before she died I had managed to spend a wonderful afternoon with her. I had called to give her a gift of oil of myrrh, which I had bought in Egypt on holiday some months earlier. We spent about four hours discussing life and death. Margaret was one of the most spiritual and selfless persons I had ever met and her life was given to looking after homeless people and other charitable works. On this occasion we also discussed how she had planned her passing, which was to be at home with her friends and family around her, and her funeral afterwards. My abiding memory of this last visit with her was of great feeling of serenity and peace as we hugged on her doorstep.

Several weeks later a mutual friend and neighbour contacted me to tell me that Margaret had passed away peacefully with her friends and family around her. Unfortunately the date of her funeral fell on the same date as the rescheduled birthday balloon holiday. I felt very sad that I would not be able to go to Margaret's funeral, but I also knew that Margaret would understand and would want me to go on holiday as planned. My mind made up, I had the sudden inspiration to do something unusual by which to remember her. I therefore planned to scatter rose petals from the balloon over the Cotswold countryside.

I informed my neighbour that I was unable to go to the funeral, and told her how I wanted to honour Margaret in a special way by scattering rose petals from the balloon. I was stunned by what my neighbour next told me. Unknown to me, the Cotswolds was an area that was very dear to Margaret and she had often visited there as a child! I had no idea that Margaret had any connection whatsoever to the Cotswolds! I asked my neighbour if she would please collect an order of service from the funeral for me as a keepsake, which she readily agreed to do.

A few days later we left for our short break in the hope that on this occasion we would be able to complete the long-awaited balloon ride. On the morning of 6 July 2010 (also the date of Margaret's funeral) we were staying in bed-and-breakfast accommodation in a beautiful and peaceful Gloucestershire farmhouse, and as I was getting myself ready in the bathroom, a gorgeous red butterfly flew in through the open bathroom window and perched on the net cur-tains for a couple of minutes before flying out of the window again. I recall feeling a great sense of peace and awe of his beautiful creature and immediately my thoughts were of the friend I had lost.

We went out that morning into a nearby village for lunch prior to our balloon ride, and I visited the florist shop where the shopkeeper kindly agreed to make up a box of fresh rose petals. Later that afternoon, the weather was beautiful and our champagne balloon ride went ahead as planned. The view was spectacular from a mile up, and, having asked permission from our 'pilot' and with a glass of champagne in hand, I scattered the rose petals over the beautiful and serene Cotswold landscape, watching them scatter to the wind before dropping slowly to earth. This was one of the most spiritual moments of my life and I will cherish this memory for ever.

On our return home a few days later I had an overpow-ering urge to play our very underused piano. (I cannot read music and I play by ear!) The music was running constantly through my mind as if on a loop was that of a hymn called 'How Great Thou Art'. I picked the tune out note by note on the piano and then played this hymn over and over for no apparent reason for the whole afternoon! The following day I called on my neighbour to ask whether she had managed to collect a copy of the order of service from the funeral. She had, and taking the booklet home with me I settled down to read it. And with tears streaming down my face I opened it to the first page on which was printed, in full, the words to the hymn 'How Great Thou Art'.

Karen is convinced that her dear friend reached out to her from the other side through a series of stunning coincidences, and the spiritual significance of coincidence also can't be ignored in this next story, sent to me by Lynn.

26 October

Last Friday I was at the supermarket looking at candle lanterns, when a boy standing next to me asked if I thought they were windproof as he wanted to put one on his girlfriend's grave. I said how sorry I was to hear he had lost his girlfriend and he went on to tell me that her name was Laura and she had died very suddenly of an aneurysm on 26 October.

I carried on to the checkout and got chatting to a woman in her sixties who had her granddaughter with her. She told me that her grandson had recently died and she was buying her granddaughter some treats to cheer her up. I again said

I was very sorry to hear such sad news. She said that the little boy had been stillborn on 26 October. I said that I too had had a stillborn baby twenty years ago, so I had a bit of an insight as to what she was going through. As I finished speaking a voice to my right said, 'Hello, Lynn.' I turned around to see my friend Mike. I must have looked shocked to see him as he said, 'What's up, you look like you have seen a ghost?' The reason for my shock was the conversation I had just had with the woman in front of me as Mike and his wife also had a stillborn baby a few years ago.

What are the chances of meeting three people in the space of fifteen minutes who have all lost someone on 26 October?

Here is Alison's story.

July

Mum died of an enlarged heart and high blood pressure and it broke my heart and my sister's too. In April this year my family and I decided to scatter Mum's ashes over an old castle ruin in Staffordshire. It overlooked where Mum used to live and she often spoke of this castle ruin. My sister and I asked for some kind of a sign. It was a lovely day with blue skies. As soon as we had scattered Mum's ashes and walked down the hill it started hailing. It was amazing. Well, we were laughing all the way down. I told my sister there was her sign from Mum. Then we heard one loud clap of thunder and laughed again. It was as if Mum was saying don't be sad.

We got home and for some reason I wanted a picture of the castle ruin, even though I had a photograph. I thought this was strange, and then this voice in my head told me to look at my calendar. Every year I buy a calendar with English scenery. I thought this was odd thinking of that as I wouldn't be buying a calendar till next year and I knew it wasn't on the one I had. I reluctantly looked at my calendar and there on the month of July (next month) was a huge picture of my mum's castle ruin. I couldn't believe my eyes and had to look at the back of the calendar to make sure it was the same place. The best thing is that July is my birthday month. It is amazing after such sadness that this message made me smile again. Some people might think I knew the picture was there but I honestly didn't.

Yes, signs can easily be dismissed as coincidences or random chance, but, even if we allow our rational minds to dismiss them in this way, there is always a part of us that knows they are far more than that. I have absolutely no objection to logical explanations for signs because everyone is entitled to their opinion – as long as that opinion does not exclude the equally viable possibility that spirits can and do speak to us through signs and the magic of coincidence.

Ask for a sign

There has been a lot of ground covered in this chapter, but my intention was to give you an overview of some of the most common – or should I say uncommon? – signs or symbols from the afterlife. If you want proof of the afterlife, one way to start is to ask for a sign. Then, the next time you have a problem or want comfort or reassurance, pay close attention to what is going on around you. You may see a feather, a cloud shape, a significant word, phrase or number over and over again, or you may hear and see signs that have unique, personal significance and meaning only for you.

In the years following my mother's death I often asked her to send me a sign from the other side, but it took many years after her death before I could allow myself to surrender my analytic mind and controlling nature and believe that what I was experiencing was heaven-sent. I needed to open myself up to the subtle signs from the afterlife that were all around me and before I could do that I needed to let go of preconceived ideas about how she might reveal herself to me. I had to understand that there is no right or wrong way to communicate with the world of spirit and I probably wasn't going to experience a full-blown visitation. I had to understand that she would reveal herself to me in ways that were highly personal and I didn't need to be psychic, a clairvoyant or a medium to communicate with her. And communicate to me she did, through subtle, gentle signs such as the appearance of white feathers, clouds, revealing dreams or coincidences at exactly the right time to guide or inspire me.

As we saw at the start of this chapter, when it comes to definitive evidence or proof of the existence of an afterlife, signs just aren't in the same league as near-death experiences. But what I'm talking about here is scientific proof or something that can be proven beyond a shadow of doubt. What happens in a person's heart is different. The heart does not need a scientific reason for everything it feels. The heart simply knows. And in all the stories you have read in this chapter the hearts of the people told them – gave them all the proof they needed – that there is another reality beyond this life and we are spiritual beings in human form. The clouds of materialism, fear and doubt melted away, enabling them to catch a glimpse of a profound truth that gave them a sense of safety and comfort they had not known before.

Maybe there has been a similar moment in your life when this great spiritual awareness and truth dawned on you. If you don't think you have seen spirits or actual evidence of the afterlife, remember that many of the people here did not actually see their deceased loved ones. Something as simple as a feather, a bird or a small coin or stunning coincidence was the catalyst for their spiritual transformation. And, if you look at the world with an open mind and heart, every moment could be a chance for you to glimpse your own unique signs from the other side. The world of spirit is always there. It may not be visible but it is still there if you look out for it and start to notice the signs. And remember to pay close attention to feelings of wonder because, whenever you feel awe, heaven is only a heartbeat away.

Hopefully, by now you may be close to accepting that there is more to this world than meets the eye. You will appreciate that strange and wonderful things can and do happen in this world and, if something can happen, it exists. It is real. And, if you are still thinking that the only possible explanation is random chance, perhaps you might like to consider the possibility that coincidence could be the language that heaven speaks.

Invisible friends

There is a category of stories that I feel I must mention before this chapter comes to a close, as this book would be incomplete without them, and these are stories about children. I've already mentioned near-death experiences involving children and at this point I'd also like to talk about children who appear to have the ability to see, hear or sense spirits. Surveys suggest that as many as one child in five has an imaginary friend. I'm well aware that many of you reading this will be thinking that imaginary friends are just that – imaginary – and I don't disagree that imagination is the most likely explanation in some cases. But then there are extraordinary cases when the imagination explanation isn't good enough – stories like this one sent to me by Grace.

Pinch of Salt

I had several miscarriages and each cut me deeply. They cut my mother even deeper, as she was longing to have a grandchild. She was also very worried about me and I think a part of her wanted me to stop trying for a baby. You see, her youngest sister, my aunt, had died in childbirth and my other aunt – her eldest sister – had become seriously ill and almost died during her pregnancy. She survived but her baby was born with severe handicaps and needed round-the-clock care. So when I announced that I was pregnant yet again I wasn't sure how my mother and grandmother would take the news.

Instead of looking anxious though my grandmother just smiled and told me that the pregnancy was a blessing and the reason why things happen as they do would become clear to me one day. When I started to bleed in the early days of my pregnancy I was confined to bed rest. I suffered the foulest morning sickness but eventually passed the magic three-month mark. I'd never made it past ten weeks before. Something felt different about this pregnancy. I could just feel it. When I was about five months gone my grandmother fell ill and within weeks her condition was critical. My mum stayed with her and I visited when I could but it wasn't easy as any stress or strain could have spelled danger for the baby growing inside me.

When I was thirty-four weeks I had a terrible scare. I thought I had gone into labour. I rushed to hospital with my husband but was told that everything was fine. I hadn't gone into labour. When I got home the saddest news was waiting for me on the answerphone: Grandma had died. Heavy with grief, as I had loved my grandmother dearly, and heavy with child, I carried my baby for another four weeks.

Monica – named after my grandmother – was born healthy and beautiful and she had the largest pair of eyes I had ever seen on a baby. They immediately reminded me of my grandmother's eyes. When she was two years old she was in the kitchen with me one day. I was baking some spaghetti bolognaise and she just came out and said, 'Pinch of salt.' I asked her what she meant and she told me that the nanny who looked after her at night always told her that everything tasted better with a pinch of salt. I was so shocked – as I remember Linda Watson-Brown always saying that to me when I was a child and used to watch her cooking – that I dropped the bolognaise sauce bowl on the floor. Monica howled with laughter.

About a week later when I was doing the housework Monica asked me to play some beetle music. Slow to catch on and thinking about insects I didn't know what she meant at first but when I questioned her she told me that her nanny liked to hear the beetles. Then it dawned on me that when she did the housework Grandma always used to play the Beatles. Intrigued by this night nanny, I asked her to tell me about her. She told me that she was such a funny lady with the 'bestest smile' and was her special friend because they had the same name and were born on the same day.

There were more instances like this in the months and years ahead, which convinced me that Monica was communicating with my grandma. It all stopped when she was about six. I'm not sure what it all means as obviously children are going to have certain traits that resemble their grandparents and great grandparents but at the time she seemed to know things about Grandma I never told her.

Linda sent me this rather marvellous story.

Dancing Lady

I want to tell you about something my husband and myself experienced roughly six and a half years ago. My sister Jackie was a very poorly lady and had been for a number of years. She could never have children of her own, which left her devastated as she adored all her nephews and nieces. Anyway, my daughter gave birth to a beautiful baby girl called Alix. She was born in November 2001. Due to my sister's ill health she could not go to see the baby but told me that when she felt better it would be the first thing she would do. Then on 2 March 2002 my sister sadly died suddenly at the age of forty. She never got to see baby Alix.

Then one day when Alix was about thirteen months old she was in her highchair in the kitchen with my husband and myself having lunch (as we were babysitting). She lost interest in her food and started to stare at the ceiling. We asked her what she was looking at and she said, 'Look Dad Dad' (she couldn't say granddad). 'Look at the pretty lady dancing.' And she kept saying that the lady was smiling and waving at her. This happened several times again over the next few weeks. Then, three months later when my daughter and I took Alix to town, we got her a few sweets in a bag to hold in her hand. She suddenly said that we needed to give the dancing lady some sweets too.

Alix is eight this year and nothing has happened since. I forgot to mention that I put a large picture of Alix in my sister's coffin and I truly believe it was my sister that Alix saw all those years ago. She had come to visit her as she promised me she would. It comforts me a lot to think that my sister is dancing in the afterlife – something she rarely got to do in this life due to her poor health.

Norbury, whom we met earlier (see 'Nearby'), also sent me this story.

Hi hi then

I have two experiences I wish to share with you. Firstly, my grandfather died when my son was about fifteen months old, and as we lived a fair way away I never got to see him much as it was. It was some time after his death when my son started watching (being transfixed [to]) certain parts of the house and was totally focused on what was there. Our son has autism and there have been many times where he has had friends that he speaks to. On this particular occasion as he was playing, he looked up at me and simply said, 'Hi hi then,' with the biggest grin on his face. My partner and I just looked at each other dumbfounded. This was my grandfather's way of saying hello and goodbye when he visited someone. My son had no real way of knowing or certainly remembering this!

And here is an account from Michelle.

Waving

Two years after my beloved dad died I gave birth to my first child (a daughter). Up until then I always felt my dad's presence with me and as soon as she was born it was like he disappeared, as if he wasn't needed any more. However, there have been numerous occasions when I've been at my mum's house and my daughter waves towards my dad's old chair (which no one ever sat in except him) and smiles as if she can see someone she knows. When we call her name she doesn't even acknowledge us. It's almost like she's in a trance and fixated on one spot. My dad always used to go on about how he would have loved grandchildren and what he'd do. He adored children and used to work with them.

My daughter is two years old now and hasn't really done the waving thing for ages now, but will still often go into a dream world and fixate on a spot and not hear us speaking to her, or she will babble quite often to me about a man that I assume she's saying she's seen or knows. But I obviously can't fully understand what she's saying as she's young still. Other strange things I've heard are, when she's been put in her bedroom for being naughty, she will be throwing a massive tantrum with screaming and crying then next minute she's laughing and chatting and saying hello as if she's talking to someone.

Psychologists argue that invisible friends in childhood are a phase or introduced because a child feels lonely in some way, but stories like those above show that there is a very real possibility that the child is actually seeing someone adults can't see. And it is not just young children who may have the ability to see spirits: many new mothers have written to me to tell me that they think their babies are seeing things that adults can't see. They talk about their babies abruptly and inexplicably stopping feeding even when they are hungry to stare at a blank wall or babbling contentedly to a fixed spot on the ceiling.

Natalie sent me this short message about her son.

Say Hello

It started when he was about six months old. He would smile at empty spaces in the room and appear to be talking to someone as I could hear him over his baby monitor babbling away and giggling. Also as he got older and could form words better we moved to a new flat and the same thing happened here as well. He is almost two now and he will look up at the ceiling in my bedroom where the light is and wave and say hello.

According to the laws of physics there are many things in our world that we can't perceive with our human senses but know are there. Many scientists now agree that existence is multi-dimensional and what we see, hear and feel isn't all that there is. Seen in this light, it is very possible that young children with receptive minds and hearts have the ability to perceive realms of existence that adults have closed their minds to, but then, as these children get older and we repeatedly tell them that they are imagining things in their efforts to fit in and please us, they lose their ability to see the world through 'angel eyes'. We should instead encourage children to trust their intuition and imagination just as we should also try to keep the child within us alive because I truly believe it is the open, trusting, spontaneous and loving nature of the child within us that is our direct link to heaven.

Four-legged friends

Talking about open, trusting natures, I also wouldn't feel that this book would be complete without at least briefly mentioning a unique category of afterlife encounters: those involving pets. For many people – myself included – losing the unconditional love of a beloved pet can leave a person feeling as tormented and alone as when a family member dies, and the comfort that a visit from a deceased pet in spirit can bring is profound. However, even those who believe in an afterlife for humans may be dismissive of animal ghosts or spirits. It is often said that animals don't have souls or spirits, so cannot survive death as humans do, but animals are made of the same energy as humans are and have the same spark of life that humans do, and I can't think of any reason why they would not survive death in the same way.

Lynette sent me this story

Tigerlily

I had a few different cats in my life but the one who was closest to me definitely had a psychic connection with me. She always knew when I was due home either from work or being out somewhere, even though those times were irregular. She fretted when I wasn't there, we shared a very close bond and she gave me such comfort and joy. Having my cats helped me so much through the break-up of my twenty-year marriage.

Eight years ago a friend gave me two kittens, a brother

and sister from the same litter. They were both adorable and I named them Tigerlily and Freddie. Tigerlily was a tiger-striped tabby and she and I became inseparable. She was my constant companion for seven years and both cats came with me when I moved from Australia to New Zealand. Two months after I arrived in NZ she suddenly became ill and passed over (in spite of the best efforts of the vets) and I've never felt such grief. Even now, ten months later, I still cry over losing her.

Since I lost her she has come to me several times in dreams and we've spent time together in the dream state. Once I woke up to feel her lying on my feet, although, when I looked, nothing was there. I've also felt the bed dip down as if she was jumping onto it, just like she used to do when it was bedtime. I feel as though she is reassuring me that she is in another form now and she is okay and wants to comfort me. I still have my grey tabby Freddie and he is a great comfort to me. He also grieved for Tigerlily as they had never been apart from when they were born. Losing Tigerlily has strengthened our bond and that's what she would have wanted.

Andrew certainly believes that his beloved cat, Poe, hasn't said goodbye and never will. Here is his story.

Passing Through

It was asking for trouble, naming a black cat Poe. But unlike the eponymous feline in the master of macabre's [Edgar

Allan Poe's] chilling tale, 'The Black Cat', my Poe returned to comfort and inspire me.

Far from being gloomy and moody, Poe was my little ray of sunshine. A friendlier, more agreeable cat I have yet to meet. I only had fifteen short months with him. One summer and one Christmas to share and treasure, that was all. He died in my arms after being hit by a car, and how quickly it was over. In despair, I watched the light go out of his eyes. My Poe was gone.

Or so I thought! Life may have been finished with Poe, but Poe was not finished with life! I cried day and night. I could hardly speak, words sticking in my throat as I choked on grief. And then something wonderful and totally unexpected happened. My Poe came back to me in spirit form. I was sitting in my conservatory, totally consumed by grief, when the room suddenly filled with Poe's presence. It was just as though he had walked into the room. It was so strong that I reached down, half expecting to touch fur. At once, I felt cheered and heartened. I hadn't been looking for this; hadn't willed it to happen. Poe himself chose his moment to come back to me, to ease my devastation. I should have known that such a loving cat would not just leave me grieving.

Something told me to go out into the garden. As I did so, I was almost knocked off my feet by the strength of Poe's presence. I quickly realised that my little angel had become part of nature. He was now in everything around me. He was in the grass, the flowers, the sun, the rain, the wind that shook the barley and the whispering trees. I knew in that instant that whenever I wanted to feel close to Poe, all I had to do was go to some natural place and there he'd be.

I'd always kept an open mind about paranormal phenomena. I'd retained an interest and had always acknowledged that inexplicable things happen to ordinary people, but what was behind it all, I'd never been sure. The events of the months following the loss of dear Poe convinced me beyond doubt that there is life after death and that the spirits of our lost loved ones regularly visit us; no question about that.

Thank you, Andrew and Poe, from the bottom of my heart, as I know this story will resonate with people who have loved and lost their precious pets everywhere!

There is no doubt that stories about animal spirits or encounters are remarkably similar to those involving encounters with departed people and, having researched both human and animal spirit stories, I have absolutely no hesitation in stating that stories about the spirits of animals are just as common as those of humans. I've read hundreds of reports of people who have seen, smelled, sensed, heard or felt the spirits of their recently departed pets. Some people report repeated visits from their pets in spirit but most of the encounters tend to happen only once, as if the animal has returned for one last goodbye. In much the same way as for the stories involving the spirits of departed loved ones in this book, all the people who have written to me say that the encounter, however brief, gave them great comfort, helped them overcome feelings of grief and allowed them to look forward again. Sandra sent me this story.

Going on

Regarding after-death experiences with animals, I was visited by my little Jack Russell, Ginny, a few weeks after she died. It broke my heart when she died, even though I knew that, just like humans, animals 'go on'.

I had woken one morning, and was just thinking about getting up to get ready for work, although my eyes were still closed. I was completely awake though. I suddenly felt the familiar 'thump' on the bed, made by Ginny jumping up. I could see her so clearly with my eyes closed, and her little face laughing at me. I reached out my hand and I felt her physically and actually stroked her warm little body. For about thirty seconds, I just lay and stroked her and then her physical presence gradually faded. I must emphasise that, even though I kept my eyes closed, I was fully awake.

Another lovely experience I was privileged to share happened when my reiki practitioner, Tracy, lost her old dog, Charlie (a girl, despite the name!). I hadn't even known she had a dog, but when I went for my monthly appointment, she told me that she was a bit upset, as one of her customers had more or less told her that animals didn't survive death. Of course we both knew differently! A couple of days later I suddenly decided to get Tracy a book about animals in the afterlife. I went online, and there were a lot to choose from. I just chose one because I liked the cover – a photo of a golden retriever. Anyway, the book came, but I started being a bit doubtful as to whether or not to give it to Tracy. Was it too soon? Would she be offended etc.? In the end I decided to stick with my first instinct and gave her the book after my next reiki session.

She stared at the cover for a moment, and then said, 'Just wait a minute' and disappeared out of the healing room. When she came back, she gave me a photograph, just saying, 'That's Charlie.' Well, the hair on the back of my neck and down my arms stood on end! The actual photo of her dog was an exact mirror image of the photo on the cover of the book! I didn't even know Charlie was a golden retriever – and the photo was an exact mirror image even down to the expression in the eyes and the turn of the head. Tracy showed the book to her daughter, who was grieving for the dog she'd grown up with, and apparently she'd been praying for a sign that Charlie was okay. Both Tracy and I believe that Charlie gave me a little nudge when I was choosing the book, knowing that it would help her family to cope with her loss.

Sceptics will naturally put down the experience of pet visitation to wishful thinking, but once again I will say that if this is the case wouldn't everyone who had loved and lost a beloved pet and dearly wanted to see it again be reporting that their pet had returned from the grave to visit them? Some of the people who wrote to me told me that they had loved many different pets over the years, but no other pet had returned, even though they dearly wished they would. And sometimes I have been sent stories of pets returning to visit people who have absolutely no connection to them or belief in the paranormal prior to their visit.

Love, whether in human or animal form, can cross the boundaries of space and time and many people who have lost beloved pets are convinced that their pets continue to visit them in spirit. After my cat Crystal died I would often sense her presence or feel the brush of her body against my legs. The experiences never alarmed me – quite the opposite: they seemed to be the most natural and comforting thing in the world. And the more I hear stories from people with similar experiences the more I am convinced that contact with a pet in spirit is possible.

Perhaps the most heartwarming thing about a pet visitation is the promise it brings that death isn't goodbye at all and one day there will be a reunion in the afterlife. And, although I haven't covered pet loss in nearly enough depth here, if you are a pet owner I hope what you have read will have shown you that when your beloved pet eventually dies – although you can't physically touch it any more – the bond between you and your pet has not broken and never will. You will simply experience it in a different way. Your pet will stay alive in your heart and in the belief that in spirit form it can be with you more intensely than before.

Turn the page

And now that I've discussed signs, briefly mentioned children who can see spirits and discussed pet visitations, it's time now for me to start summing up all the evidence I have gathered together for you so far. In the next and final chapter, I would like to present concluding arguments for my unshakable conviction that death is not the end and heaven is real. So, if you are ready to open your mind and listen with your heart, please turn over the page.

CHAPTER SEVEN

Heaven is Real

Death is like taking off a heavy winter overcoat in the spring when we don't need it any more.

Elizabeth Kubler-Ross

Throughout this book I have tried in the best way I can to present my case for the very real existence of an afterlife. In the early chapters I offered you perhaps my strongest evidence, or proof, with a discussion of near-death experiences, and then moved on to eyewitness reports from ordinary people who believe they have actually seen, heard or encountered spirits. I've shown that afterlife encounters can happen at any time but they are more likely to happen when a person is grieving the loss of a loved one, and when the experience happens it is a source of tremendous comfort and relief. I have also shown that in the vast majority of cases the experience was spontaneous. In other words, the person did not actively seek contact with a departed loved.

I hope I have also made it clear that afterlife encounters can happen to anyone regardless of their age, background or spiritual or religious beliefs. Heaven does not discriminate and psychic experiences are far more widespread and common than you might think. So, if you have had what you believe may be an afterlife encounter and are worried others might laugh at you, think you are crazy or losing it, I hope you will realise that you are not alone. You are in very fine company indeed.

Scientific evidence

I'm aware that the majority of the evidence I have presented is anecdotal and based on witness statements, and this is because I believe that personal accounts are the most powerful and convincing evidence we have. But I want to strengthen my case further by briefly summarising some of the latest scientific evidence for the existence of an afterlife.

At the onset I want to point out that there is far more hard evidence out there for the existence of heaven than you may realise, and this hard evidence comes from a variety of different and well-documented case studies, research projects and reports. A number of Nobel Prize-winning scientists, including Marie Curie, Max Planck, Erwin Schrödinger, Charles Richet and Brian Josephson, have examined this evidence and concluded that certain supernatural phenomena are real and simply cannot be authenticated by conventional scientific explanations.

I've already devoted a chapter to near-death experiences but perhaps I didn't fully stress there how hard scientists have tried and failed to explain the phenomenon of a person leaving their dead or dying body and discovering information that could not even have been detected with their normal senses, and later that information is found to be 100 per cent correct. Science and medicine just can't explain this and other characteristics of near-death experiences, which all clearly point to the startling conclusion that the mind, or consciousness, can exist independently of the brain. Conventional science has always believed that the mind and the brain are the same but the latest research is suggesting otherwise. Increasing numbers of doctors and scientists are acknowledging the startling possibility that consciousness can exist independent of reality and by so doing they are acknowledging the possible existence of a spiritual realm. And neither can scientists explain how, around the time of death, spirits of the dead have appeared in different locations to people who sometimes don't even know that a loved one was dying or even in danger of dying. Then there are documented cases of shared deathbed visions when a person sees the same spirits as the dying person, not to mention tangible evidence provided by ghostly images caught on cameras as well as EVP recordings (see 'Calling out to me' in Chapter 5).

And, as if all this weren't enough, there have also been a number of scientific studies on the phenomenon of mediumship. A medium is someone who claims to be able to communicate directly with the dead. I made a conscious decision to avoid stories about mediums or psychics in this book as the subject is so vast and I don't feel I could do it justice here. I also felt that mediums have had a lot of negative press over the years due to the fact that there are a lot of people who are preying on the grief of the gullible for financial gain. There are, however, some rare individuals who do seem to have extraordinary powers and some of these individuals have allowed themselves to be tested scientifically.

As you might suspect, the idea that a person can at will communicate with the dead has been routinely dismissed by scientists in centuries past but in recent years mediumship has gradually started to emerge as a valid subject for controlled experiments and academic research. Scientists in prestigious universities all over the world have started to investigate the work of certain mediums, and their investigations have produced some overwhelmingly positive results.

One leading researcher in the field of mediumship studies is Professor Gary Schwartz of the Laboratory for Advances in Consciousness and Health at the University of Arizona. Schwartz is quoted (in an article written by Danny Penman about the paranormal for www.newsmonster.co.uk) as stating that he believes, 'Some mediums are real ... we've proved it experimentally ... these mediums are getting accurate information. We've convincingly ruled out every one of the conventional, sceptical explanations ... some mediums really are getting accurate information and only people who do not know the research or ignore the evidence could come to any other conclusion.' And Patricia Robertson and astrophysicist Emeritus Professor Archie Roy from Glasgow University, who conducted their own research into whether mediums could talk to the dead, both agree with Schwartz's evaluation. In Robertson's words, 'There is no doubt about it. Mediumship works. We are convinced that some mediums can impart to a sitter information about people who have died that they can't possibly know in any normally accepted way.' Robertson goes on to say that this is not to suggest that the information is coming from the dead but in her opinion that is the most plausible explanation. Also in agreement is Dr Peter Fenwick, a neuro-psychiatrist from King's College London, who believes that the most logical explanation for the work of mediums with a high accuracy rate in controlled experiments is that they are genuinely communicating with the dead. And this is to name but a few.

Sceptics are convinced that other explanations can be found and that scientists who have studied mediums and have come to the conclusion that their work is genuine are misguided in their interpretation of events. Despite this, an increasing number of academics and scientists are coming to very different conclusions indeed and there remain many people who have found unmatched comfort and reassurance following a visit to a psychic. People like Joy, whose story follows on below.

Messages

A clot took Dad in the end, which was a blessing, as his death would not have been pleasant by all accounts. The funeral was at the church where Mum and Dad were married. The vicar was new to the area, and didn't really know Dad well enough and the service felt empty. Mum and I decided the next time to visit the Spiritualist church.

My granddad came through first with a message for my mum when we went to the Spiritualist church and had a

meeting with a medium. Mum and I were very emotional –
this was our first experience of mediums and receiving messages – but nevertheless, we were both extremely calm,
albeit emotional. The medium said to Mum, 'You were looking for papers in a wooden inlaid box last night and were
asking, Why my husband? Why not someone who was horrible and deserved to die? You threw the box lid across the
bed, and sobbed and sobbed.' My mum, nodded, and said yes
and no, with her mouth at times open. I'm thinking wooden
inlaid box, also thinking Mum too polite to say, No, this wasn't
a message for me. Although I enjoyed the tranquillity, the
friendliness and atmosphere, which was almost like being in
your own front room and not in any way a church with dead-
pan faces, I couldn't help but think the message wasn't meant
for Mum. We had our cuppa, chatted to some of the people
there and left, saying we would see them next Sunday.

I sat in the car, turned to Mum and asked her what she
thought. She told me that the medium was absolutely spot
on and that she had looked for papers the night before. She
had sobbed and asked, 'Why my husband?' and thrown the
wooden inlaid box lid across the bed. I asked what inlaid
box, and Mum told me that my father had made it when he
was an apprentice and they kept a bit of cash and insurance
policies etc. in it under a floorboard in a cupboard in front
of which was a set of drawers on casters (casters put on by
Dad for ease of movement for Mum). For many, many years
thereafter, we received other wonderful messages through
mediums from the spirit world, which helped us all to come
to terms with losing our dad at such an early age.

That was my first experience of mediumship. I've had several others but one of the most dramatic was when my mum came through. After Mum died I was extremely upset and felt I had let her down by not being with her at the end. I couldn't get it out of my head and decided to go to the Spiritualist church with my husband.

I hadn't been to the Spiritualist church for a good while, but was greeted with open arms, which set me off crying again. Within seconds of the medium linking in with spirit, she came to my husband explaining that she would speak to him, as I was clearly very upset. She didn't ask if Mum had just passed away, she just instinctively knew. She said that Mum wanted to thank me and the family for looking after her and for the beautiful flowers on the coffin and the replica for the interment. It was then that the penny dropped: without even thinking about it I had chosen real flowers that Mum would have loved for the coffin.

Although this helped, I still felt I'd let Mum down. I drank my cuppa after the service had ended. The medium was still on the stage drinking hers when I took my cup and saucer to the kitchen. The medium asked me to come and sit down for a minute as I passed by because she still had a link with my mum. She said that I was understandably extremely upset because I'd lost Mum but I should stop beating myself up. She then said my dad was talking about a cigar. I said we had been clearing bits and bobs out and found a cigar we had bought for him thirty years ago from the USA had disintegrated so we had had to throw it away.

The medium then said, 'Have you heard people saying

the whole family has congregated round the dying relative's bed at home or hospital and after a while one would go to the loo, one would go for a cigarette, another for a shower, or to feed the kids or animals while the dying person falls asleep and when they return their loved one has passed away? Your mum is saying it is one thing to be there for her, living with her, feeding her, loving her, laughing with her, crying with her, but for you to experience her taking her last breath was not what she wanted.'

At that moment, a great burden was lifted from my shoulders. I thank the universe for introducing me to spirituality. Of course, you never ever forget, or stop completely grieving for those you have lost, but it would be unbearable as far as I'm concerned if I didn't believe that one day we will all be together again.

I've visited a medium only once and it was a frustrating experience, but I have many friends who have visited mediums and they are convinced they have been offered real evidence that a departed loved one is close by, because the medium gets everything right and knows things they couldn't possibly know. And when this happens, as Joy mentioned in her story above, nothing can be more reassuring.

You may wonder why I have visited a medium only once given the nature of my work as a writer on the paranormal, and the reason for this is that I don't feel the need to. I don't doubt that there are a number of gifted mediums out there who could give me more proof that afterlife communication is possible, but the message of all my writing is that you don't need to contact a medium to talk to the departed. All the stories in my books show that there is an abundance of evidence that supports the idea that ordinary people – people like you and me, who don't think they have great psychic powers – can make contact with loved ones in spirit, without consulting a so-called expert or doing anything out of the ordinary. I'm not saying here that I am condemning mediums, because I don't, because I have seen the miracles they can sometimes work. I am just saying it is not for me and it is not something I would typically recommend, as it is direct, personal contact with the other side without the need for intermediaries that is my passion.

Before I move away from the topic of mediumship, I'd like to add that it is not just everyday people who are finding information gathered from a psychic extremely helpful: there have also been documented incidences of mediums helping detectives when murders can't be solved in the usual way. There are also a large number of mediumship reports and studies that have been gathered by scientists and researchers that have not been made fully known to the public. The only reason I'm not discussing more of these studies in this book is that I am not a scientist and I did not conduct the experiments. However, if you do want to take a look at the subject from a scientific and academic point of view, you will discover, as I did, that the evidence for the existence of an afterlife is overwhelming. (You will find lots of suggestions for further reading and research on mediumship – as well as for the academic research and case studies I mentioned earlier – at the end of the book.)

Scientific evidence aside, I have no doubt that some of you may still find it extremely hard to accept the idea that heaven exists and the human spirit survives death. I completely respect your opinion. However, I'm sure you will agree that a lot of the stories in this book are very hard to explain and in the majority of cases stress, intense grief, wishful thinking or imagination are not definitive explanations. It would also be very closed-minded at the very least not even to consider the possibility that some part of us may be able to transcend the barriers of time and space and survive bodily death – not even to consider the possibility that the spark of life inside us is eternal or that there are spiritual forces at work within and around us.

Indeed, when you start stacking up all the evidence from the work of mediums to near-death experiences, out-of-body experiences, visitations, deathbed visions and other forms of after-death communication, it all begins to point to one life-changing conclusion: death is not the end. When you look at all this impressive evidence, ask yourself whether it is easier to believe that every one of these experiences has been a mistake, a fraud or a hallucination or whether it is actually more logical and reasonable to believe that there could be life after death.

Again, as this book draws to a close, I can't offer you definite proof, but all I can say is that all the people whose stories are in this book – and all the millions of people around the world who have reported similar experiences – are in no doubt that what they experienced was genuine. They know that they glimpsed a world that was as real and as profound as their everyday lives and that this glimpse of spirit was a milestone – a turning point – in their lives. It gave them hope and comfort that the spirit lives on and by so doing helps them to accept the loss of a loved one and move beyond their grief.

Season of grief

Those who have experienced an afterlife encounter feel that it helps them establish a new relationship with their deceased loved ones. It also gives them great comfort and hope, helping them move forward with their lives. However, I'm well aware that many people reading this book may not have had a visitation or afterlife encounter and may still be grieving the loss of a loved one. If this is the case I hope reading this book will help change your understanding of life and death and reassure you that when you are ready you can enter into a new relationship with a departed loved one. Even though you can't physically touch or hug them any more you can still experience them in a different way. They can stay alive in your heart and mind and be with you more intensely than ever before. Before that transformation happens, though, there must be a season of grief.

Many people who have recently lost a loved one ask me why they can't see or sense that person around them. My answer is that, before spirits can reach out to us, there needs to be a period of grief and acceptance of the passing. Spirit finds it hard to break through feelings of intense guilt, fear, pain and anger. They act like a barrier and for many people it is only when they are able to come to terms with physical loss, and feel stronger emotionally, that spirits can appear. But how do you come to that acceptance?

I don't claim to be a bereavement counsellor but I do know that the first step is to experience your time of grief. You have to grieve and you have to mourn. You have to understand that grieving for the loss of a loved one does not mean you have no faith in an afterlife. It just means you are human and missing physical contact and the way your life used to be before someone you loved died. Just as a mother experiences the pain of labour before the joy of birth you must go through the pain of grief before you can experience the joy of reunion in spirit.

Understanding the grief process can help. It won't stop the pain but it will reduce fear, because you will know that experiencing an explosive and bitter range of emotions is common. You will understand that the initial response is denial and shock followed by feelings of anger, guilt, helplessness and futility: anger at your loved one for leaving you; guilt because you don't think you did or said all that you wanted to say; helplessness and futility because you realise that there are some things in life you can never control. Terrifying as these feelings can be, try to remember that they are neither good nor bad – just feelings. If you don't work through these feelings – allow them to happen – physical symptoms, such as insomnia and headaches, may occur and the chances of serious depression increase. If this is the case, it is vital that you talk to your doctor or to a grief counsellor.

Although there are common responses to grief, it is important to bear in mind that we all go through the various stages of grief differently and for some the season of grief may be far longer than for others. There aren't any right or wrong ways to experience grief, and you need to give yourself the time that you need because grieving can't be hurried. Broken hearts – like broken bones – take their own time to heal. There aren't any quick remedies or cures and at times you may wonder if you will ever pull through, but you must allow yourself to grieve. Remember, it is fine to cry or feel angry. If you need to scream, then scream out loud. You are not going crazy. You are a human experiencing painful loss.

Unless you have always been incredibly self-sufficient and find comfort in your own company, getting as much help and support from loved ones or friends can prove crucial when you are in the process of grieving. If you were ill you would be cared for by friends, family or your doctor, so never be afraid to ask for support from those who care about you, or, if you feel you need to seek help outside family and friends, those who can help you professionally. It goes without saying that taking care of yourself by eating well, exercising and getting enough sleep and treating yourself in the way your loved one would have taken care of you if they were alive can all ease the pain, as can keeping in touch with the world around you.

Should you feel worthless and guilty because you are alive and your loved one is not, try to remember that it was your loved one's time to cross over and not your time to leave this life yet. You are a unique and wonderful person and there is a reason and a purpose to your life on earth. Perhaps one day you will help someone else move through and beyond their grief. The suffering you have experienced can strengthen you and make you more compassionate, gentle and understanding towards others. Your perspective on life can improve and trivial incidents and material concerns can lose their power to unsettle you. Your suffering can therefore be regarded as an experience that forces you to grow spiritually and to live your life more fully and meaningfully. Growth after all is the reason for your existence in both this life and the next. You are here to grow in understanding and love. You are here to grow spirituality.

Working through your grief will take time, sometimes a very long time, but trust me, because I have lost people I thought I could not live without. The pain does fade and it will get easier to bear. Eventually and slowly, your life will get back on track and, when feelings of sadness strike, they won't fill you with panic and dread any more, because you know you will survive. You will have more good days than bad days and you will come to understand that there is life beyond death, but it will be a new life for you and a new relationship with your loved one in spirit. You will know that your loved one lives on for ever in your heart and that, when you call on them, they will hear you loud and clear. Hoping for things to go back to normal after the death of a loved one isn't realistic, because your life has been changed for ever by your loss. Now your choice is to make this change either a positive or a negative one. You can choose to live in sadness and pain or you can choose to live your life to the full. It is obvious which approach to life your loved one would have preferred you to take, and what better memorial to them than to celebrate the life you shared? And bear in mind that, just as you have your life to live, those in spirit have to adjust to their life, too, and, if you obsess too much about them and can't move forward with your life, they can't move forward in spirit either. This doesn't mean you should never think about them – that would be terrible – but just that the greatest love in both this life and the next is the love that can set a spirit free.

Remember, moving beyond grief is not about denial but about remembering your loved one without feelings of intense pain shattering your life. It is about coming to a place where memories of your loved one are sweet and gentle. It is about

Patient: Ellie Mackay   90001753

Appointments:

Thursday, 21 May 2015 12:00 - Aberdeen Orthodontics

We charge for late cancellations & missed appointments.

Aberd
230-2
Aber
C

(9000

reclaiming the part of yourself you gave away. When you love someone you give a part of yourself to that person, and this 'giving away' is one of the most magical things about love, as long as you don't take it to extremes. If you give away too much of yourself, this isn't healthy for them or you, because it is confusing love with need. True love, as we have seen, is love that can set a spirit free and when a loved one dies, amid all the pain, your loved one is giving you the opportunity to take back the part of yourself that you gave away. This won't happen overnight, but if you give yourself plenty of time to grieve you will eventually find that the passion and love you gave away returns to you. You will rediscover what true love really is and how it can make you feel whole again.

It can be hard to understand but the death of a loved one can lead to greater self-love and an awakening of spirit if you allow yourself to work through your season of grief. This is certainly what has happened to me. It was only several years after my mother died – when I had gone through all the stages of grief – that I realised that the only thing left was this overwhelming feeling that the love I had for my mother and the love she had for me had not died. This love was alive and was watching over me from the other side.

When you are ready

If you haven't had an after-death communication, you may be wondering at this point why not. Every week I get letters or emails from people asking me why they haven't seen, sensed or heard a much-loved friend or family member who has passed over. They wonder if this is somehow their fault or if their loved one doesn't care enough about them to make contact. They are in desperate need of comfort and reassurance but don't feel they are receiving any.

There are some rare people who have psychic eyes and can see the world of spirit with ease, but, as I always say in my books, I have never been one of them and I suspect there are many people out there like me who have often felt that heaven is far away. This was especially the case when my mother died and, try as I might, I couldn't make contact with her. I didn't know what was wrong with me and it was especially difficult because I grew up in a family of spiritualists and many of my friends were accustomed to having paranormal experiences.

One school of thought suggests that intense feelings of guilt and loss make it hard for spirits to contact us – and this was probably the case for me when my mother died – but in my research I have found that this is not always the case. Some people wrote to me about encounters they had experienced in deep states of grief. Others suggest that trying too hard may be the problem. Again, that may have been the case for me but, then, I have also had stories from people who begged for a sign following the death of a loved one and received one. Nor is it essential for people to believe in life after death, because a number of stories are from sceptics who, prior to their experience, had no belief whatsoever.

I really don't know why it is easier for some people to catch a glimpse of heaven than others. I can only say that in my case I needed some kind of shock to see the light. Following my mother's death I hit rock bottom. I questioned and doubted everything I had ever believed in and then, when I least expected it or even hoped for it, I started to hear her call my name. She began to appear to me in vivid dreams and flashes of insight and inspiration. For some reason I needed a shock to trigger a sense of urgency and that shock manifested in the form of doubt and depression – doubting everything I thought I knew and the depression and feelings of darkness and emptiness that ensued. I truly lived and breathed the words of the philosopher Albert Camus when he wrote, 'In the depth of winter, I found there was in me an invincible summer.'

For other people it may not be the loss of a loved one or a questioning of beliefs that prompts a re-evaluation of their lives. It could be a relationship breaking down or a job loss or anything that forces a dramatic rethink about what really matters to them. But light and spiritual growth and understanding need not always come out of the depths of darkness. As we've seen in this book, spiritual awareness and growth can be inspired by a wonderful coincidence, the beauty of nature, the smile of a child, the hug of a loved one, the sound of beautiful music or any moment of private magic that triggers a profound realisation that there *has* to be more to this life than the physical.

Whatever the trigger may be for you, rest assured that, when you are ready, you will see, hear or sense the world of spirit and connect with those you have loved and lost. If you don't think you can see anything, be patient because you will one day. Perhaps there is more for your spirit to learn and experience before you catch a glimpse of heaven. Don't try to pressure or

Theresa Cheung

rush yourself: just live your life with love and goodness and honesty. This doesn't mean becoming religious or trying to be perfect – that is impossible, because to be human is to be imperfect – it means living in a way that you feel those who have crossed over to the other side would approve of.

I'm often asked if there is anything a person can do to increase the chances of an afterlife encounter. A relaxed and open state of mind that is willing to suspend disbelief can certainly increase the likelihood. Some people can achieve this state through meditation or relaxation techniques, while others do it through simple things like walking in the countryside or creative work. And others can simply achieve it through doing work they love or surrounding themselves with people they love. It is during periods of quiet contemplation and dedication like this that people often discover that they are more than just their physical bodies. They instinctively understand that they are not defined by their bodies and minds and not even by their feelings and thoughts. They have an identity that exists independently of their humanity, and awareness of this spiritual identity gives them a feeling of deep inner peace and bliss. They instinctively know that material gains and goals – the acquisition of money, wealth and power – are not the path to true happiness and that it is not what you have but who you are and what you do with your life that matters. Another way to increase the chances of communication is to ask for a sign and then to wait patiently and notice what happens. That sign may be a feather, a rainbow, a memorable dream, or it may be something deeply personal that only you can understand.

And you may not realise it, but simply reading this book can act as a catalyst. If you have found the evidence I have offered you intriguing and exciting, then your heart and mind are opening and your chances of having an encounter yourself will increase significantly. If you can think of this book as your arrow to heaven, I wouldn't be surprised if you receive a message, sign or even vision from the other side in the near future. And when you do please write to me about it – details about how to do so can be found on page 256 I would love to hear from you.

The great unknown

Death ends a life, not a relationship.

Jack Lemmon

I suspect that one of the reasons we fear death is that it is the great unknown – the final mystery. Even though I have always had a strong belief in the afterlife I am willing to admit that the thought of death still scares me, but the many wonderful stories I have read over the years about near-death experiences and visions of heaven, as well as communication with departed loved ones in spirit, have reassured me and taken the sting out of death. I have come to understand that it is not death I am afraid of but fear of the greatest change of all – fear of leaving my physical body behind and living a new life in spirit. However, whenever I get anxious about dying I simply reread the wonderful stories I have included in this book and others like them and any uncertainty and fear I have about death are replaced with a newfound sense of hope and peace. I am reassured that death is nothing to fear because there is a part of us that doesn't die. There is life after death. We are just passing through. There is always more than meets the eye.

Over the centuries scientists and researcher have tried to understand or define life. They have studied living and nonliving organisms and tried to highlight the differences, and it seems that cell walls and chromosomes that can reproduce or replicate are the defining features. So they have tried to create artificial life forms with transported cell walls and chromosomes using electrical shocks and other devices. The problem is, these artificial life forms can never be classified 'alive' in the sense that they have intelligence and feelings. There is something unseen or invisible that gives organisms life, and that is something scientists cannot create in a lab. For me, this unseen power or force is the invisible life force of spirit – the part of us that simply cannot die.

If you think about it the failed attempts of scientists to create artificial life may be the best proof of all that death does not exist. Yes, your physical body may die when your heart stops beating but the unseen part of you remains, the part of you that exists in the hearts of other people. Death is therefore not the end of life, just your spirit leaving your body. The essence of you survives and, if you have ever lost someone you love, a part of you will already know that this is true. It is hard to describe, but somewhere deep down you know that person is still alive within you and all around you. If you have ever seen the body of a departed loved one this is especially the case. I remember when I used to work in an old people's home as a care assistant. I would often be in the room following the death of a resident. I would look at that person's body and it really did seem like the essence of that person had gone. Their dead body looked like a familiar outfit or clothes that were not being worn any more. The resident I remembered and had interacted with previously had gone. Their body was not them.

Death is something we don't like to think or talk about and for that reason it is surrounded by mystery, but I hope this book has shown you that death is a natural process and it can be as beautiful and magical an event as birth. It is simply another phase in your existence, and your life continues on the other side. Seen in this spiritual light death is not something that should be feared. It is hate, fear, anger and guilt that kill, not death. Death is a heart devoid of love, compassion and good-ness and for those who live in spirit there can be no death because love and goodness keep their spirits alive.

Viewed in this spiritual light death should not be an occasion for great sorrow or anguish. Yes, of course we miss physical con-tact and weep for that, but we should also rejoice that a loved one's spirit has learned valuable life lessons and is now ready to move on to a life in spirit. In some cultures funerals are not depressing affairs, as they tend to be in the West, but occasions for great celebration and we could all learn from that. I've been sent quite a few stories from people who have seen departed loved ones attend their own funeral and many of them say that the spirits would much rather see friends and relatives and loved ones attending the funeral smile and celebrate their lives. They don't like seeing tears at their own funerals, as this next story from Jessica illustrates so well.

I Did Not Die

After reading your book this week I wanted to write to you to tell you about something magical that happened to me at my son John's funeral. The service was beautiful and I was drowning in tears. His death wasn't entirely unexpected as we had known for years that one day the cancer would take him from us, but you can never really prepare yourself to bury your child, can you?

I felt lost and not sure how life would be without having to think about taking care of John. In the last year he had been so ill that my every thought had been taken up by him. We got to the point in the service when [the poem] 'Do Not Stand at My Grave and Weep' was read out by John's brother and I'm telling you, Theresa, I saw John standing next to his brother. He was nodding and smiling at me. He looked radiantly happy and healthy and he looked so alive that I turned around to my sister and asked her if she could see John too. She shook her head and just put her arm around me. I think she thought it was my grief talking but it wasn't. John was there – at his own funeral. As soon as the poem ended John faded away slowly. His feet went first and then his arms and finally there was just his smiling face and then that disappeared too.

I'm not saying I haven't had some dark days since John died and I still cry an awful lot, but when I am at my lowest I think back to what I saw at the funeral and it gives me great strength.

Jessica's story didn't include the full version of the famous poem mentioned but I am going to include a version of it (for there are several) here as in my research file I have a dozen stories referencing this poem being read out at funerals and those attending feeling a deep sense of understanding, comfort and warmth when the words are read.

> Do not stand at my grave and weep,
> I am not there; I do not sleep.
> I am a thousand winds that blow,
> I am the diamond glint on snow,
> I am the sunlight on ripened grain,
> I am the gentle autumn rain.
> When you wake in the morning hush
> I am the swift uplifting rush
> Of quiet birds in circling flight.
> I am the soft stars that shine at night.
> Do not stand at my grave and cry,
> I am not there; I did not die.

If I had my way, this poem believed to be by Mary Frye would be a compulsory reading at all funerals, because it remains one of the most simple but powerful expressions of comfort and hope for those grieving the loss of a loved one.

Remember, you don't need to see visions of departed loved ones or have a near-death experience to discover spiritual meaning in your life. As you've probably noticed in this book, there are many opportunities in everyday life to discover awareness or a deep realisation that you are more than the physical body you live in. This realisation may come through personal tragedy or crisis, but it may also come in subtler, gentle ways, through heavenly music or the words of a beautiful poem, like the one above, or through an unexpected feeling or thought, an answer to a prayer, an insightful dream; or it could come through a surge of joy or a sign that speaks personally and directly to your heart and reminds you of the nearness of those who have crossed over and the true meaning of your life. Often it is through simple, unexplained feelings and experiences that heaven shines through and reminds us of something we may have forgotten along the way – this life is not all that there is. Humble experiences like this one described so simply but so profoundly by Olivia.

Crying and Smiling

I was sitting in a car that was following my husband's coffin on its way to the graveyard. One moment I was in tears and then the next moment – out of nowhere – I felt a surge of joy and peace I have never known before or since. In that moment I felt warm and comforted. It gave me strength and hope. I knew that I would see my beloved husband again. I thought I would never be able to smile again but smiling felt like the most natural thing in the world.

When a moment of profound realisation of the eternal truth of life comes to you, as it did to Olivia, you become a source of hope and comfort to others. You become the meaning and the messages others are consciously or unconsciously seeking, because they see spiritual strength and light within you and what they see imprints itself on their hearts, reawakening spirit within them.

So, if the stories in this book about contact with deceased loved ones have spoken directly to your heart, you now have a clear choice. You can doubt and question what you have read or you can let it change your life for ever and the lives of all those lucky enough to cross your path. You can turn away from the light or you can bask in the warmth, joy and certainty that are eternal life in spirit. And if you choose the light – as I hope you will – you may not realise it but you are playing a vital part in transforming the world for the better.

Sadly, the world we live in today is troubled and often unjust and violent, and many people feel helpless to change that, but the greater the belief in an afterlife, and that we are all on a spiritual journey together, the greater understanding, respect and tolerance for each other we will have. The more that people understand that life is eternal and that love conquers fear, hatred, anger and death, the more peaceful and enlightened this world will become. And it can all start with you and the choices you make with your heart. It all starts with your becoming the change you want to see in the world.

All the stories in this book teach us that the only thing that matters in life is what goes on in your heart and, from what I have read and understood, it seems to me that the sole purpose of our life on earth is to learn the true value of unconditional love and compassion towards ourselves and others. What, then, is the purpose of death? Why do innocent people or children have to die while others perhaps less deserving live long and productive lives? Perhaps the purpose of this life is to learn spiritual lessons, and maybe some souls need only a few days, months or years to learn their lessons – or teach others lessons – while others take a little longer.

I don't have all the answers, and perhaps it is best that we don't know the reason for everything that happens on earth, because, if we knew why some people suffer or why injustice and cruelty take place in the world, we would not reach out to each other. Think about it. We know why a woman cries out in pain when she gives birth to a child and because we know why she is suffering we don't get too concerned or worried. If we knew why others suffered perhaps we would be less compassionate, and in terms of our spiritual development that would be an abhorrent existence – death in its truest sense.

Keeping it real

Life and death are one, even as the river and the sea are one. In the depths of your hopes and desires lies your silent knowledge of the beyond; and like seeds dreaming beneath the snow, your heart dreams of spring. Trust the dreams, for in them is hidden the gate to eternity.

Kahlil Gibran

Thank you for reading this book. I truly hope it has convinced you that the afterlife is real but, if it hasn't entirely, at the very least I hope it has unlocked your mind to the possibility that a part of us survives when we die. Remember, keeping an open mind is essential because only when our minds are open can we progress and evolve as a human race. It really wasn't so long ago that most people truly believed that the earth was flat. It was thought that if you ventured too far you would fall off the edge of the world. It was only when a few courageous few opened their minds, questioned that assumption and returned with stories of what they had seen beyond the horizon that people slowly began to accept that the end of the world had existed only in their own minds. Today, most people still fear sailing beyond the horizon of life into death. They think of it as the end of their existence, but the stories in this book show that this is not the case. They show that after death a wonderful new life awaits us. They show that death is only something that exists in our own minds and all we have to do to remove the fear of death is stop believing in it.

If you have read this book with an open heart and mind you will know that there is no death. All that happens is a transformation, a change from a physical state to a spiritual state, rather as a caterpillar transforms into a butterfly. A part of you has always known this eternal truth but may have forgotten it amid all the chaos and confusion of the material world.

That's why, as we reach the final few lines of this book, you may be feeling that what you have read sounds somehow familiar, as if you know it all already. This is because the stories in this book offer glimpses into a real spiritual dimension you have lived in before and where you will one day return when your time on earth is complete. They offer glances into a world of wonder and beauty, where all those who have crossed over before you are living in eternal love, joy and peace. They reveal to you a place that your heart instinctively recognises as your true spiritual home.

Listen to your heart.

It always knows what is real.

AN INVITATION – AND
FURTHER READING AND RESOURCES

The more we talk openly about afterlife encounters the more comfort and hope it will bring to others grieving the loss of a loved one, so, if you have had a visitation or night vision from a beloved person or animal or an afterlife encounter or experience of any kind and would like to share your story, please get in touch with me. I would love to hear from you and, if possible, to include your story in a future book. To send me a story or just get in touch, you can visit my website http://www.theresacheung.com, or write to me care of Simon and Schuster, 1st Floor, 222 Gray's Inn Road, London WC1X 8HB.

Further reading and research

Listed below are books, case studies and articles written by scientists, psychologists, doctors, parapsychologists and researchers, as well as some prominent afterlife research organisations and websites. They can all provide strong, scientific and case-study evidence that can be put forward to support the conclusion drawn in this book that the afterlife is real. If you do decide to read further you will immediately see that I could have included a great deal more solid scientific evidence and well-known case studies in this book, but I chose not to because I feel strongly that the most powerful and convincing evidence for life after death is the true stories sent to me by ordinary people.

Allen, Edward, 2007, *The Survival Files: The most convincing evidence yet compiled for the survival of the soul* (Moment Point Media).

Almeder, Robert, 1987, *Beyond Death: Evidence for Life after Death* (Thomas).

Barrett, William, 2011, *Deathbed Visions* (White Crow)

Bayless, Raymond, 1973, Apparitions and survival after death (University Books)

Browne, Mary, 1997, *Life after Death* (Ivy Books)

Calvi-Parisetti, Piero, 21 Days into the Afterlife (free e-book available at http://www.openmindsite.com).

Cheung, Theresa 2006, *The Element Encyclopedia of the Psychic World* (Harper Element).

Cooper, Callum, 2012, *Telephone Calls from the Dead* (Tricorn Books).

Crookes, William, 2012, *Researches into the Phenomenon of Spiritualism* (Forgotten Books).

Fontana, David, 2005, *Is There an Afterlife? A Comprehensive Review of the Evidence* (O Books).

Fontana, David, 2009, *Life Beyond Death: What should we expect?* (Watkins Publishing).

Gauld, Alan, 1983, *Mediumship and Survival: A century of investigations* (Flamingo).

Grosso, Michael, 2004, *Experiencing the Next World Now* (Pocket Books).

Grosso, Michael, 1976, 'The survival of personality in a mind-dependent world', *Journal of the American Society for Psychical Research*, 73, pp. 367–80.

Theresa Cheung

Gurney, Edmund, 2011, *Phantasms of the Living* (Cambridge Library Collection: Spiritualism).

Hude, Anna, *The Evidence for Communication with the Dead* (free E book available on http://www.openlibrary.org).

Hyslop, James, 2012, *Contact with the Other World: The latest evidence* (Forgotten Books).

Iverson, Jeffrey, 1992, *In Search of the Dead: A Scientific Investigation of Evidence of Life after Death* (BBC Books).

Keen, Montague, 2011, *The Scole Report: An Account of an Investigation into the Genuineness of a Range of Physical Phenomena Associated with a Mediumistic Group in Norfolk, England* (Saturday Night Press).

Respected paranormal researcher Montague Keen also gathered together a list of twenty cases that he believed conclusively proved the existence of life after death. His list was based on a similar list originally published by Professor Archie Roy in *The Paranormal Review*, a magazine published by the Society of Psychical Research. Here's that list:

1. The Watseka Wonder, 1887. Stevens, E. W., 1887, 'The Watseka Wonder, Chicago', Religio-philosophical Publishing House; and Hodgson, R., *Religio-Philosophical Journal*, 20 December 1890, investigated by Dr Hodgson.

2. Uttara Huddar and Sharada. Stevenson, I., and Pasricha, S., 1980, 'A preliminary report on an unusual case of the reincarnation type with Xenoglossy', *Journal of the American Society for Psychical Research* 74, pp. 331–48; and Akolkar, V. V., 'Search for Sharada: Report of a case and its investigation', *Journal of the American Society for Psychical* Research 86, pp. 209–47.

3. Sumitra and Shiva-Tripathy. Stevenson, I., Pasricha, S., and McLean-Rice, N., 1989, 'A Case of the Possession Type in

India with Evidence of Paranormal Knowledge', *Journal of the Society for Scientific Exploration* 3, pp. 81–101.

4. Jasbir Lal Jat. Stevenson, I., 1974, *Twenty Cases Suggestive of Reincarnation* (2nd edn) (University Press of Virginia).

5. The Thompson/Gifford case. Hyslop, J. H., 1909, 'A Case of Veridical Hallucinations', *Proceedings of American Society for Psychical Research* 3, pp. 1–469.

6. Past-life regression. Tarazi, L., 1990, 'An Unusual Case of Hypnotic Regression with some Unexplained Contents', *Journal of the American Society for Psychical Research*, 84, pp. 309–44.

7. Cross-correspondence communications. Balfour, J., 1958–60, 'The Palm Sunday Case: New Light On an Old Love Story', *Proceedings of the Society for Psychical Research* 52, pp. 79–267.

8. Book and Newspaper Tests. Thomas, C. D., 1935, 'A Proxy Case extending over Eleven Sittings with Mrs Osborne Leonard', *Proceedings of the Society for Psychical Research* 43, pp. 439–519.

9. 'Bim's' book-test. Glenconnor, Lady, 1921, *The Earthen Vessel* (John Lane).

10. The Harry Stockbridge communicator. Gauld, A., 1966–72, 'A Series of Drop-in Communicators', *Proceedings of the Society for Psychical Research* 55, pp. 273–340.

11. The Bobby Newlove case. Thomas, C. D., 1935, 'A proxy case extending over Eleven Sittings with Mrs. Osborne Leonard', *Proceedings of the Society for Psychical Research* 43, pp. 439–519.

12. The Runki missing-leg case. Haraldsson, E., and Stevenson, I., 1975, 'A Communicator of the Drop-in Type in Iceland: the case of Runolfur Runolfsson', *Journal of the American Society for Psychical Research* 69, pp. 33–59.

Theresa Cheung

13. The Beidermann drop-in case. Gauld, A., 1966–72, 'A Series of Drop-in Communicators', *Proceedings of the Society for Psychical Research* 55, pp. 273–340.
14. The death of Gudmundur Magnusson. Haraldsson, E., and Stevenson, I., 1975, 'A Communicator of the Drop-in Type in Iceland: the case of Gudni Magnusson', *Journal of the American Society for Psychical Research* 69, pp. 245–61.
15. Identification of deceased officer. Lodge, O., 1916, *Raymond, or Life and Death* (Methuen & Co. Ltd.).
16. Mediumistic evidence of the Vandy death. Gay, K., 1957, 'The Case of Edgar Vandy', *Journal of the Society for Psychical Research* 39, pp. 1–64; Mackenzie, A., 1971, 'An Edgar Vandy Proxy Sitting', *Journal of the Society for Psychical Research* 46, pp. 166–73; Keen, M., 2002, 'The case of Edgar Vandy: Defending the Evidence', *Journal of the Society for Psychical Research* 64, issue 3, pp. 247–59; Letters, 2003, *Journal of the Society for Psychical Research* 67, issue 3, pp. 221–4.
17. Mrs Leonore Piper and the George 'Pelham' communicator. Hodgson, R., 1897–8, 'A Further Record of Observations of Certain Phenomena of Trance', *Proceedings of the Society for Psychical Research*, 13, pp. 284–582.
18. Messages from 'Mrs Willett' to her sons. Cummins, G., 1965, *Swan on a Black Sea* (Routledge and Kegan Paul).
19. Ghostly aeroplane phenomena. Fuller, J. G., 1981, *The Airmen Who Would Not Die* (Souvenir Press).
20. Intelligent responses via two mediums: the Lethe case. Piddington, J. G., 1910, 'Three incidents from the Sittings', *Proceedings of the Society for Psychical Research* 24, pp. 86–143; Lodge, O., 1911, 'Evidence of Classical Scholarship and of Cross-Correspondence in some New

Automatic Writing', *Proceedings of the Society for Psychical Research* 25, 129–42.

Kubler-Ross, Elizabeth, 2009, *On Death and Dying* (Routledge).

Lagrand, Louis, 1997, *After Death Communication Final Farewell: Extraordinary Experiences of Those Mourning the Death of Loved Ones* (Llewellyn, 1997).

Lodge, Oliver, 2010, *Life and Death: Evidence for survival after death* (Biblio Bazaar).

Long, Jeffrey, 2010, *Evidence of the Afterlife: The Science of Near-death Experiences* (Harper Element).

Moody, Raymond, 2001, *Life after Life: Survival of Bodily Death* (Rider).

Morse, Melvin, and Terry, Paul, 1992, *Closer to the Light: Learning from the near-death experiences of children* (Ivy Books).

Myers, F. W. H., 2012, *Human Personality and Its Survival after Death* (Forgotten Books).

Newton, Michael, 1994, *Journey of Souls: Case studies of lives between lives* (Llewelyn).

Osis, Karlis, 2006, *At the Hour of Death* (Hastings House).

Radin, Dean, 1997, *The Conscious Universe: The Scientific Truth of Psychic Phenomena* (Harperone).

Raudive, Konstantin, 1971, *Breakthrough: An Amazing Experiment in Electronic Communication with the Dead* (Colin Smyth).

Richet, Charles, 2003, *Thirty Years of Psychical Research* (Kessinger Publishing, LLC).

Ring, Kenneth, 1982, *Life at Death: A Scientific Investigation of Near-death Experiences* (William Morrow).

Rogo, D. Scott, 2006, *Life After Death: The Case for Survival after Bodily Death* (Guild Publishing).

Sabom, Michael, 1982, *Recollections of Death: A Medical Investigation* (Corgi).

Sabom, Michael, 1998, *Light and Death: One Doctor's Fascinating Account of Near-Death Experiences* (Zondervan).

Sage, Michael, 2012, *Mrs Piper and the Society of Psychical Research* (Tredition).

Schwartz, Gary, and Beischel, Julie, 2007, 'Anomalous Information Reception by Research Mediums Demonstrated Using a Novel triple-Blind Protocol', *Explore*, January 3, Issue 1, pp. 23–7.

Sullivan, Robert, 2012, *Angels on the Night Shift: True stories from the ER* (Harvest House).

Thomas, Charles, 2006, *Life beyond Death with Evidence* (Read Books).

Tymn, Michael, 2001, *The Afterlife Revealed; What happens after we die* (White Crow).

Underwood, Peter, 1994, *Ghosts and How to See Them* (Anaya Publishers).

Wallace, Alfred, 2009, *Miracles and Modern Spiritualism* (Cambridge University Press).

Zammit, Victor, *A Lawyer Presents the Case for the Afterlife* (free E book at http://www.victorzammit.com).

Organisations

Association for the Scientific Study of Anomalous Phenomena: An organisation that promotes an open-minded, scientific approach to the study of unexplained phenomena and the results of all investigations are published. A training programme is provided to encourage members to undertake their investigations in a disciplined and responsible way. Website: www.assap.org.

College of Psychic Studies: The college was founded 125 years ago by a group of eminent scholars and scientists with the purpose of formally investigating psychic and mediumistic phenomena. Today, the college has evolved to incorporate the more general exploration of a consciousness beyond matter and it offers a number of courses, lectures and workshops in spiritual matters. Website: http://www.collegeofpsychicstudies.co.uk.

Cruise Bereavement Care: Not in any way connected to spirituality or research into the afterlife, but a nationwide charity that exists to promote the wellbeing of bereaved people and to help anyone suffering a bereavement to understand their grief and cope with their loss. It offers confidential counselling and support and advice about practical matters. Website: http://www.crusebereavementcare.org.uk.

Para.Science: This group is dedicated to the serious study of all types of paranormal phenomena and makes use of the latest photographic, video and sound equipment and techniques to undertake this research. All results of investigations made can be viewed by the public. Website: http://www.parascience.org.uk.

Society for Psychical Research (SPR): The aim of the SPR is to scientifically investigate and understand events and abilities typically described as psychic or paranormal. The Society promotes and supports academic research and publishes scholarly papers. It also organises educational events and has an annual conference. It also publishes the *Journal of the Society for Psychical Research* – a quarterly publication with scholarly research and case studies. Website: www.spr.ac.uk and, for the American Society, www.aspr.com.

Spiritualist Association of Great Britain: The primary purpose of the Spiritualist Association of Great Britain is to offer evidence through mediumship of the continuation of the personality after physical death and to relieve suffering through Spiritual Healing. Website: http://www.sagb.org.uk.

Websites

After Death Communication Research Foundation: Devoted to afterlife experiences and the search for their meaning following the loss of a loved one. See http://www.adcrf.org.

Near Death Experience Research Foundation: See http://www.nderf.org.

Out of Body Experience Research Foundation: Dedicated to reporting and researching NDEs, OBEs and other spiritually transformative events. See http://www.oberf.org.

Two other websites worth checking out for NDE research are: http://www.aleroy.com and http://www.near-death.com/evidence.html.

And finally . . .

Research from the USA suggests that most medical doctors believe there is life after death and say that their spiritual beliefs influence how they practise medicine. In a survey of more than 1,000 doctors, 76 per cent said they believed in heaven and 59 per cent said they believed in some sort of afterlife. See http://www.msnbc.msn.com/id/8318894.

And, contrary to popular opinion, another study indicates that the more educated and intelligent a person is, the more likely they are to believe that the afterlife is real. See http://www.msnbc.msn.com/id/10950526.

Death is not extinguishing the light, it is only putting out the lamp because the dawn has come.

Rabindranath Tagore